ANNA ELIZABETH DRAEGER

Creative Designs
Using Shaped Beads

KALMBACH BOOKS

Kalmbach Books
21027 Crossroads Circle
Waukesha, Wisconsin 53186
www.Kalmbach.com/Books

Published in 2014
18 17 16 15 14   1 2 3 4 5

Manufactured in the United States of America

ISBN: 978-1-62700-052-9
EISBN: 978-1-62700-053-6

Editor: Mary Wohlgemuth
Art Director: Lisa Bergman
Technical Editor: Jane Danley Cruz
Layout Designer: Lisa Schroeder
Illustrator: Kellie Jaeger
Photographers: James Forbes, William Zuback

Publisher's Cataloging-in-Publication Data

Draeger, Anna Elizabeth, author.

   Creative designs using shaped beads / Anna Elizabeth Draeger.

      pages : color illustrations ; cm

   Issued also as an ebook.
   ISBN: 978-1-62700-052-9

   1. Beadwork–Patterns. 2. Beadwork–Handbooks, manuals, etc.
   3. Jewelry making–Handbooks, manuals, etc. I. Title.

TT860 .D7324 2014
745.594/2

Contents

Beads as building blocks

Many more shapes have emerged since my book *Great Designs for Shaped Beads was released: Rizo beads, twin and SuperDuo beads, Rulla and brick beads, gumdrops, and spikes, to name a few. Although* specialty shapes like these are unusual and inspiring, many shapes that have been around for a long time deserve attention too. Bead shapes like round (also known as rocaille), cylinder, triangles, cubes, and bugle beads have been staples for years, and their distinct shapes play an important role in designing beaded jewelry.

When we look at each bead for its individual shape advantages, its properties become like building materials in an architectural structure. That is what ties all the projects in this book together: how individual shapes combine into beautifully designed jewelry.

On the pages that follow, you'll find a section of projects devoted to each of these jewelry types: beaded beads, rings, earring, bracelets, and necklaces. Each project explores a different way of uniting two or more different bead shapes into a well-constructed and lovely piece. As you stitch your favorites, you'll discover my secrets for engineering focal beads, components, and other building blocks of design.

Anna

GUIDE TO THE BEADS

ROUND (ROCAILLE) SEED BEADS

These are the beads that usually come to mind when thinking of seed beads. Czech and Japanese seed beads are the main beads I use. These beads are made of glass, and can come on hanks of several strands or loose in bags or tubes. The quantities are usually measured in grams, and these beads tend to be the least expensive of the shapes available, although new colors and finish treatments can really bump up the cost. Common seed bead sizes for jewelry making are 15º–8º, but seed beads come in many other sizes as well. I've stuck to a very limited group of seed beads because there are just so many different ones available. Other seed beads that fall under the seed bead category are Charlottes, hex beads, pony beads, and a few more cylindrical shapes that are not Delica beads.

Round seed beads can range in size from these big 3ºs down to tiny 15ºs (upper left)

CYLINDER BEADS

Cylinder beads are like tiny tubes—cylindrical rather than round like regular seed beads. Cylinder is a generic term for Miyuki Delica beads or Toho Treasure or Aiko beads. Miyuki Delica beads come in sizes 15º, 11º, 10º, and 8º, and are wonderfully versatile. Miyuki also makes a hex version of these sizes. Toho Treasures are comparable to 11º Delicas. Toho's Aikos are the most precise and expensive cylinders available. When the generic term "cylinder bead" is used in a pattern, it means that either brand will work. Some beadwork projects specify the brand because the Toho cylinders are slightly larger than Delicas.

Cylinder beads are tiny tubes with large holes

TRIANGLE BEADS

Toho and Miyuki both produce triangle beads. Toho's triangles are sharp edged and slightly irregular. You'll end up weeding out any undesirable shapes if your design requires precision. Miyuki makes a rounder version. Both brands come in a range of sizes and a wide variety of finishes and colors. It's important to get the correct brand of triangles because the sizes vary due to the shape. Toho triangles nestle very closely to each other, and Miyuki triangles don't sit as closely due to the rounded shape.

Miyuki triangles have a soft shape and round holes

Toho's version has a crisp triangle shape and triangular hole

GUIDE TO THE BEADS

CUBE BEADS

Miyuki cubes come in sizes 1.8mm, 3mm, and 3.5mm. Toho cubes come in 1.5mm, 2mm, 3mm, and 4mm. Both brands come in a wide variety of colors and finishes. Miyuki has slightly sharper corners than Toho. Most of the time, you'll find cubes loose in tubes or bags, but I've also purchased cubes on hanks.

Miyuki cubes have round holes

Look for the square holes of Toho cubes

BUGLE BEADS

When it comes to variety, bugle beads take the cake. There are many different sizes, brands, and shapes. Bugles may be smooth and cylindrical or be twisted, spiral, hex, triangular, or square. They come on hanks, in tubes, or in bags, and in a wide range of sizes, but the most commonly used sizes in jewelry are between 3mm and 12mm. Many artists use long bugles for fringe. Some bugles are not only measured by their length, but they also come in sizes. For example, size 1=3mm, size 2=6mm, and so on. Sometimes this can be confusing. Just pay close attention to the millimeter size called for, and use calipers if needed to choose the right length.

I often use basic, tube-like bugles and twisted bugles

SPIKE BEADS

Czech pressed spike beads come in sizes 4.5x8mm, 6.5x16.5mm, and 11x18mm. They come in a wide variety of finishes and colors. In this book I've used only the small and medium sizes of these cool beads.

MAGATAMA BEADS

Magatama beads are sometimes referred to as drop beads, and so they can be easily confused with long drops.

LONG DROP BEADS

These beads are a longer version of Miyuki's drop beads. They measure 3x5.5mm.

TILA BEADS

Tila beads are 5x5mm tile beads with two holes. The name is pronounced TEE-la. Miyuki makes Tila beads in a large variety of colors.

Tilas are smaller, slimmer, and sharper-edged than Czech tiles

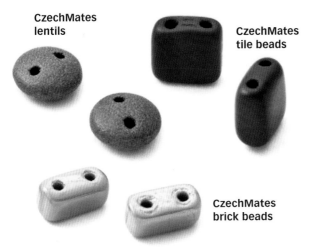

CzechMates lentils

CzechMates tile beads

CzechMates brick beads

CZECHMATES

CzechMates is a line of two-hole pressed glass beads made in the Czech Republic that includes 6mm tile beads, 6mm lentil beads, and 3x6mm brick beads. All of these beads are usually quite precise, with rounded edges and even holes. Two-hole tile beads look a bit like Tila beads, but they are thicker and have rounded edges and corners. Brick beads look like tiny bricks. They have rounded edges and corners and are half as wide as the tile beads. Lentil beads are round, flat disks; CzechMate lentils have two holes.

SUPERDUO BEADS

SuperDuo beads are 2x5mm oval beads with pinched ends and a wide middle. They are well shaped and even, so aside from the occasional plugged hole, you hardly have to cull these beads. Often you'll be able to poke out a blocked hole with a beading awl, but sometimes the hole is fused shut and you'll need to discard that bead. Take the time to check both holes as you're picking up beads in a project to save you the time of taking everything apart to remove an offender later.

Two types are called SuperDuo: the one I've described above and a second, wider version. The wide version is sometimes called SuperDuo II; they will not work for the designs in this book. A third type is called Twin beads, and these will not work in my projects either. Twin beads are often uneven and need to be culled.

These Twins (left) and SuperDuo IIs (below left) are fatter than SuperDuos and don't nestle together

SuperDuos (shown in red above) have pinched ends

RIZO BEADS

Rizo beads remind me of grains of rice with a hole at one end. They come in a great variety of smooth, consistently even finishes.

Rizo beads are 2.5x6mm

GUIDE TO THE BEADS

7x8mm rose petal (front)

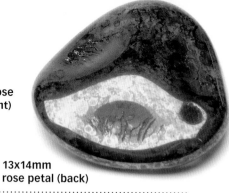

SMALL AND LARGE ROSE PETALS

These are beautiful beads with luxurious finishes. I used both sizes of rose petal beads in this book.

13x14mm rose petal (back)

side view

Gumdrops are 7x10mm

GUMDROP BEADS

Czech-made gumdrops come in many delicious colors and finishes. They are similar to spike beads but create a softer look.

16mm dagger

DAGGER BEADS

You'll find small, medium, and large dagger beads. They are Czech-made and thus are available in a beautiful range of solid colors as well as Picasso finishes.

8mm daggers

RULLA BEADS

2x5mm Rulla beads are similar to brick beads, but are rounded like a cylinder with the two holes running through the sides.

Czech-made Rulla beads

HOW TO USE THIS BOOK

To help you decide if the project is a good fit for your stitching ability and the beads you want to work with, each project includes a guide to the stitches used, the key bead shapes used, and the skill level. Within a chapter, the projects are arranged in order from beginner to advanced.

Here are my definitions of the four skill levels I used:

Beginner: This project is a great starting point. Even if you're not familiar with the noted stitches, it's no problem. They are explained in detail within the instructions and illustrations, and you should be able to jump right in.

Motivated beginner: This project is a bit more difficult than a beginner-level project, but don't let that stop you from giving it a try. If you get stuck, look at the stitches used a little more closely. The review of basic techniques that starts on p. 90 may help. Try working a practice length of the stitches until you feel more comfortable.

Intermediate: This project is for a beader who is comfortable with the techniques used. The instructions assume you've made several projects using the same stitches.

Advanced: This project is good for anyone who is comfortable with all stitches and isn't afraid to try a new and interesting way of putting them together. I may also call a project advanced if there are many different stitches being combined. Deeper understanding of the way the stitches work is helpful.

Baby Baubles

Make adorable little dimensional beads to complement a favorite strand of stone beads. Accent them with sparkling crystals for a necklace and earrings set you can wear anywhere.

BEADS

- ⬭ Rizo bead
- ◯ 11º seed bead
- ⚫ 15º seed bead

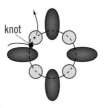

fig. 1

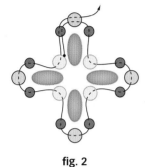

fig. 2

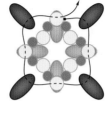

fig. 3

MATERIALS

One Baby Bauble
- **8** Rizo beads, jet Picasso
- **8** 11º seed beads, Montana luster
- **8** 15º seed beads, matte black
- Fireline 6 lb. test
- Beading needles, #12

Necklace (19 in./48cm)
- **9** Baby Baubles
- **28** 10mm oval stone beads, hematite
- **38** 3mm bicone crystals, crystal silver shade
- **58** 15º seed beads, matte black
- **2** 4–6mm jump rings
- Clasp
- **2** crimp beads
- **2** crimp covers
- Beading wire, .014
- Crimping pliers
- Wire cutters

Earrings
- **2** Baby Baubles
- **4** 3mm bicone crystals, crystal silver shade
- **2** 1½-in. (3.8cm) headpins
- **2** earring findings
- Chainnose pliers
- Roundnose pliers
- Wire cutters

1 On 24 in. (61cm) of Fireline, pick up an alternating pattern of an 11º seed bead and a Rizo bead four times, leaving a 6-in. (15cm) tail. Tie the beads into a ring with a square knot, and sew through the first 11º [**fig. 1**].

2 Pick up a 15º seed bead, an 11º, and a 15º, and sew through the next 11º in the original ring. Repeat this step three times, and then step up through the first 15º and 11º picked up in this step [**fig. 2**].

3 Pick up a Rizo bead, and sew through the center 11º in the previous round. Repeat this step three times [**fig. 3**].

4 Retrace the last round several times, work your way back through the second round, and then retrace the initial ring several times, exiting next to the tail. Tie the working thread and tail together again, and sew through the next few beads in the initial ring. End the working thread. Thread a needle on the tail, sew through a few beads in the initial ring in the opposite direction, and end the tail.

TO STRING THE NECKLACE

1 Make nine Baby Baubles.

2 Cut a 24-in. (61cm) piece of beading wire. String a crimp bead to about 1 in. (2.5cm) from the end, and then go back through the crimp bead and crimp it, leaving a loop to attach the jump ring and add the clasp.

3 String a repeating pattern of a 15º, a 3mm bicone crystal, a 15º, and an oval stone bead 10 times.

4 String a repeating pattern of a 15º, a 3mm, a Baby Bauble, a 3mm, a 15º, and a oval stone bead nine times.

5 Work as in step 3 until you have ten oval stone beads on the second half of the necklace, ending with a 15º, a 3mm, and a 15º.

6 String a crimp bead, go back through, and crimp it, making a loop the same size as the other end.

7 Open a jump ring, attach half the clasp to an end loop, and close the jump ring. Repeat on the other end.

8 Close a crimp cover over each crimp.

TO MAKE EARRINGS

1 Make two Baby Baubles.

2 On a headpin, string a 3mm bicone crystal, a Baby Bauble, and a 3mm.

3 Make a wrapped loop above the last crystal.

4 Attach an earring finding to the wrapped loop.

5 Make a second earring.

DESIGN OPTIONS

Use mini daggers or magatama long drops in place of the Rizo beads to make a variation of the Baby Baubles.

COLORS

Dagger earrings
- 3x12mm daggers, green
- 11° seed beads, green-lined crystal AB
- 15° seed beads, gunmetal iris

Teal Baby Bauble
- Rizo beads, teal AB
- 11° seed beads, green-lined crystal AB
- 15° cylinder beads, matte green

Crystal Baby Bauble
- Magatama long drops, light green-lined crystal
- 11° seed beads, gunmetal iris
- 15° cylinder beads, purple iris

Dark purple Baby Bauble
- Rizo beads, purple AB
- 11° seed beads, green-lined crystal AB
- 15° cylinder beads, purple iris

TECHNIQUES Flat and tubular peyote stitch, netting, tubular herringbone stitch

SKILL LEVEL Intermediate, working knowledge of tubular peyote helpful

Delica Delights

Create depth, dimension, and interesting geometric shapes by embellishing a basic flat peyote tube with netting and tubular peyote. Using a contrast of colors or finishes for these beads increases the impact of the embellishment.

BEADS

☐ 15º Delica bead, color A
☐ 15º Delica bead, color B

MATERIALS

Beaded bead necklace (20 in./51cm)

- **42** 4mm bicone crystals, air blue opal AB2x
- **50** 3mm bicone crystals, purple velvet
- 4 grams each of two colors of 15º Delica beads: color A, matte metallic copper; color B, copper-lined crystal
- Clasp
- Craft wire, 20-gauge, purple
- **8** jump rings, 5mm
- **6** crimp beads, copper
- Fireline, 6 lb. test
- Beading wire, .014, purple
- Beading needles, #13
- Chainnose pliers
- Roundnose pliers
- Wire cutters

Base bead

1 On 2 yd. (1.8m) of Fireline, pick up 58 color A 15º Delicas, and center them on the thread. Work in even count peyote stitch using As to make a base that is 58 beads long and 12 rows wide (that is, six beads in each offset row) **[fig. 1]**. Switch to the other thread when you run out of thread.

2 Roll the beadwork into a tube and zip up the long edges.

3 Exit an edge A and work a round of tubular herringbone (basics) off the end round using As, and step up through the first A picked up in this step **[fig. 2]**.

4 Pick up three As, and work in tubular herringbone, to make a picot at the top of each pair of beads on the edge row. Step up through the first two As picked up in this step **[fig. 3]**.

5 Repeat on the other end, and end the threads.

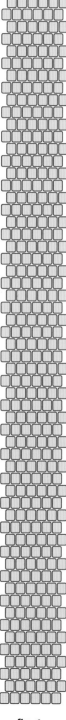

fig. 1

fig. 2

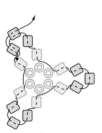

fig. 3

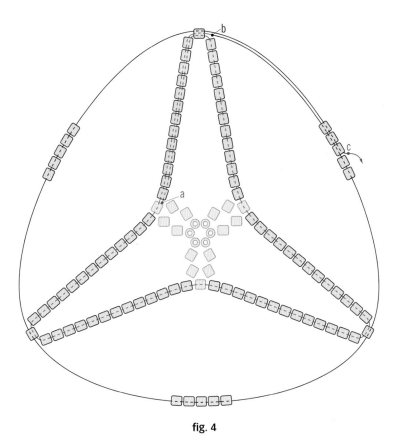

fig. 4

Embellishment

1 Add 2 yd. (1.8cm) of Fireline to one end of the base bead, and exit the center A at the top of a picot [**fig. 4, point a**]. Pick up 27 color B 15º Delica beads, and sew through the center A at the top of the next picot. Repeat the last stitch two times, and then step up through the first 14 Bs picked up [**a–b**].

2 Pick up five Bs, and sew through the 14th B in the next set of 27 in the previous round. Repeat this step two times, and then step up through the first three Bs picked up in this step [**b–c**]. This will make the embellishment start to snug up around the base bead.

3 Pick up three Bs and sew through the third B in the next set of five in the previous round. Repeat this step two times, and then step up through the first Bs picked up in this step.

4 Work in tubular peyote stitch: Pick up one B, skip a B in the previous round, and sew through the next B. Repeat to complete the round, and step up through the first B picked up in this round. Repeat to work a total of 11 rounds of tubular peyote, and remember to step up through the first bead picked up in the new round.

5 Work in tubular netting: Pick up seven Bs, skip three Bs from the previous round, and sew through the next B in the previous round. Repeat this step two times, and then step up through the first four Bs picked up in this step.

6 Continue to work in tubular netting: Pick up seven Bs per round, skip seven Bs in the previous round, and sew through the fourth B in the next set of seven in the previous round. Repeat this step four more times.

7 Work a round of tubular netting: Pick up three Bs per stitch, skip seven beads in the previous round, and step up through the first B picked up in this step.

8 Work 11 rounds in tubular peyote using Bs.

9 Work a round of netting: Pick up five Bs, skip three Bs in the previous round, and sew through the next B in the previous round. Step up through the first three Bs picked up in this step.

10 For the last round, pick up 13 Bs, and sew through the center A at the top of the next picot on the other end of the base bead. Pick up 13 Bs, skip five Bs in the previous round, and sew through the third B in the next set of five. Repeat these two stitches to complete the round, and then end the threads.

11 For a necklace, make a total of three beaded beads.

TO MAKE THE NECKLACE

1 Make a plain loop at the end of a piece of wire. String a 4mm bicone crystal, a beaded bead, and a 4mm. Make a plain loop. Repeat with the remaining beaded beads.

2 Link the beaded beads together with jump rings.

3 On 12 in. (30cm) of beading wire, string a crimp bead, a plain loop at the end of the beaded bead chain, and go back through the crimp bead. Crimp the crimp bead.

4 String five As, a 3mm bicone crystal, an A, a 4mm, an A, and a 3mm. Repeat this sequence five more times, and then string five As.

5 String a crimp bead, and go back through the crimp bead with the remaining beading wire to make a small loop. Crimp the crimp bead.

6 String five Bs, a *3mm, a B, a 4mm, a B, a 3mm, a B, a 4 mm, a B, a 3mm, a B 15, a 3mm, three 4mms, and a 3mm. Pick up a B, and repeat the sequence from the *. Pick up a B, and then pick up a 3mm, a B, a 4mm, a B, a 3mm, a B, a 4 mm, a B, a 3mm, and five Bs.

7 String a crimp bead, go through the same end loop of the beaded bead chains, and go back through the crimp bead. Crimp the crimp bead, and trim the excess wire.

8 Repeat steps 3–7 on the other end of the beaded bead chain.

9 Attach half of a clasp to each end loop of the beading wire with two jump rings.

DESIGN OPTION

Make pint-size versions of these beaded beads for bracelets or earrings. Simply start with 26 As in the first step instead of 58. Pick up 13 B Delicas in step 1 of "Embellishment" instead of 27. Work a total of three rounds of tubular peyote instead of 11, work four center netted rounds instead of six, and then make the second half of the bead as a mirror image of the first.

COLORS

- Color A 15º Delicas, gold iris
- Color B 15º Delicas, purple iris

Super Spheres

The blueprint of this beaded bead is similar to the Bugles with Crystals beads on p. 23, although it looks different. The two-hole lentil beads add another dimension that gives this bead a lot of depth and texture.

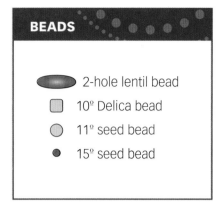

BEADS

⬭ 2-hole lentil bead

☐ 10º Delica bead

○ 11º seed bead

● 15º seed bead

fig. 1

fig. 2

fig. 3

fig. 4

fig. 5

1 On 3 yd. (2.7m) of Fireline, pick up a repeating pattern of a 15º seed bead, a 10º Delica bead, a 15º, and a lentil bead four times, leaving a 12-in. (30cm) tail. Sew through the first 15º and 10º again to form a ring.

2 Pick up three 10º's, and sew through the 10º your thread exited at the start of this step and the next 15º, lentil, 15º, and 10º. Repeat this step three more times, and then sew through the beads to exit the bottom hole of the next lentil. Change direction and step up to the top hole of the same lentil [fig. 1].

3 Pick up three 15º's, and sew through the top hole of the next lentil. Repeat this step three times, and then reinforce the beads picked up in this round by retracing the thread path, but skip the center 15º's to create a diamond shape. (This step will be repeated each time you create a lentil bead unit, but will not be shown on subsequent illustrations.) Sew through to exit the next lentil, and then change direction and step down to the bottom hole of the same lentil bead [fig. 2]. Sew through the beadwork to exit a center 10º in one of the picots.

4 Pick up a 15º and a lentil bead, a repeating pattern of a 15º, a 10º, a 15º, and a lentil three times, and then pick up a 15º. Sew through the 10º your thread exited at the start of this step, and the next 15º, lentil, 15º, and 10º.

5 Work as in step 2 to add picots to the remaining open 10º's in the bottom ring. Work as in step 3 to add the 15º's to the top round. Sew through the beadwork to exit a 10º across from the join of the previous component in the bottom round.

6 Work as in steps 3–5 to complete the third unit [fig. 3].

7 Join the beads into a ring: Exiting a center 10º in the end picot of the last unit, pick up a 15º, a lentil, a 15º, a 10º, a 15º, a lentil, and a 15º. Sew through the center 10º of the end picot of the first unit. Pick up a 15º, a lentil, a 15º, a 10º, a 15º, a lentil, and a 15º, and sew through the 10º your thread exited at the start of this step [fig. 4]. Work as in step 2 to complete the two remaining picots needed, and then work step 3.

8 Exit a center 10º from a picot along either edge of the ring. Pick up a 15º, a lentil, a 15º, and sew through the center 10º from the next picot along this edge. Repeat three more times [fig. 5], and then sew through the next lentil. Sew through the remaining hole of the same lentil to change direction, and then work step 3.

9 Exit an open side 10º in one of the picots. Pick up a 10º, and sew through the nearest side 10º in the next picot. Repeat two more times, and then sew through the new 10º's just added [fig. 6]. Sew through the next opening between three lentil units. Repeat this step three more times on this side of the bead.

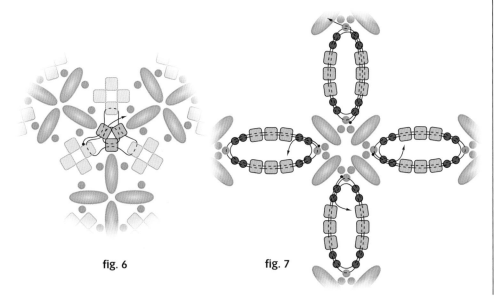

fig. 6

fig. 7

MATERIALS

Blue beaded bead

- **24** 2-hole lentil beads, blue iris

- 2–3 grams 10° Delica beads, silk satin gray

- 2–3 grams 11° seed beads, transparent-lined blue rainbow

- 2–3 grams 15° seed beads, blue iris

- Fireline 6 lb. test

- Beading needles, #12

Violet/gray beaded bead colors

- Lentil beads, purple iris

- 10° Delica beads, matte gray

- 15° seed beads, lavender permanent finish

10 Sew through the beadwork to exit a center 10° from a picot on the other edge of the ring. Repeat steps 8 and 9 on the other edge of the bead.

11 Exit a center 15° between two lentils in any lentil unit, pick up two 15°s, three 11° seed beads, and two 15°s. Sew through the center 15° of a set across from where your thread just exited. Pick up two 15°s, three 11°s,

and two 15°s, and sew through the 15° your thread exited at the start of this step. Retrace the thread path, skipping the center 15°s to pull the beads into an oval shape [**fig. 7**]. Sew through the beadwork to exit the center 15° in the next stitch.

12 Repeat step 11 to complete all four oval seed bead embellishments off of this set of lentils,

and then sew through the beadwork to exit the center 15° in the next set of lentils. Continue working in this manner until all of the sets of lentils have been embellished with oval seed bead embellishments.

13 Retrace any loose thread paths, and end the threads.

DESIGN OPTIONS

Use SuperDuo beads in place of the lentil beads, and use contrasting colors to make the bottom and top layers really stand out. Another design option is to use 2mm round crystals or another color of 11° seed beads to add one more design element. Exit a center 11° from the oval seed bead embellishment, and pick up a 2mm or 11°. Sew through the center 11° from the nearest oval embellishment. Repeat two more times to create a little sparkling accent between each group of three oval embellishments (see gold/copper bead).

COLORS

Gold/copper bead

- SuperDuo beads, matte metallic copper

- 11° seed beads: color A, metallic silver; color B, matte metallic gold

- 15° seed beads, matte metallic gold

- 2mm round crystals (optional embellishments)

Ivory/bronze bead

- SuperDuo Beads, opaque white Picasso

- 11° seed beads, matte metallic silver

- 15° seed beads, metallic brown

Blue/purple bead

- SuperDuo Beads, transparent light blue luster

- 11° seed beads, galvanized lavender

- 15° seed beads, matte metallic blue iris

Bumble Beads

Love gumdrops? Stitch a single sweet beaded bead or make a playful statement with a group.

MATERIALS
Necklace (19 in./48cm)
- **18** gumdrops, green/bronze
- **8** 4mm bicone crystals, olivine
- 6–7 grams peanut beads, light green luster
- 3 grams 11º seed beads, light green-lined crystal AB
- 3–4 grams 15º seed beads, brown iris
- Clasp
- **2** crimp beads
- Fireline, 6 lb. test
- Beading wire, .014
- Beading needles
- Crimping pliers
- Wire cutters

Bronze bead colors
- Gumdrop beads, metallic bronze
- 11º seed beads, matte burgundy
- 15º seed beads, transparent amber AB

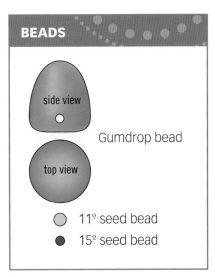

BEADS

side view

top view

Gumdrop bead

○ 11º seed bead

● 15º seed bead

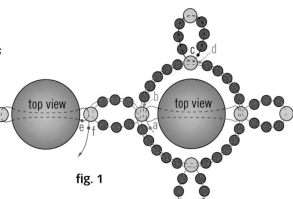

fig. 1

1. On 2 yd. (1.8m) of Fireline, pick up an 11º seed bead, a gumdrop, and an 11º, leaving a 6-in. (15cm) tail. Sew back through the gumdrop and the first 11º picked up so that the working thread and tail exit opposite sides of the same bead [**fig. 1, a–b**].

2. Pick up five 15º seed beads, an 11º, and five 15ºs. Sew through the 11º on the opposite side of the gumdrop. Repeat this step.

3. Sew through the next five 15ºs and the following 11º [**b–c**], pick up three 15ºs, an 11º, and three 15ºs, and then sew through the 11º again [**c–d**]. Repeat this step three times, and then sew through the first three 15ºs and 11º picked up in the last repeat [**d–e**].

4. Pick up a gumdrop and an 11º. Sew back through the gumdrop and the 11º your thread exited at the start of this step [**e–f**]. Sew back through the gumdrop and the 11º.

DESIGN OPTIONS

Make these beads really stand out by using 7x17mm spike beads. Add another dimension by using Rizo beads in place of the 11º seed beads in step 8. Because the spikes are a little more narrow at the base than gumdrops, you may have to add another round of seed beads around each base to make the spikes snug: Exit one of the 11ºs surrounding a spike. Pick up a 15º, an 11º, and a 15º, and sew through the next 11º in the ring. Repeat three times, and then sew through the first three beads picked up. Pick up an 11º or a 15º, and sew through the next three beads. Repeat three times, and then sew through the beadwork to exit an 11º surrounding another spike. Continue in this manner until all the spikes are secure.

COLORS
Burgundy/tan spike bead
- spike beads, matte chalk bronze lumi
- 11º seed beads, matte burgundy
- 15º seed beads, brown iris

COLORS
Black/silver spike bead
- Spike beads, black silver Picasso
- Rizo beads (in place of 11º seed beads in step 11), black silver Picasso
- 11º seed beads, metallic teal green
- 15º seed beads, nickel plated

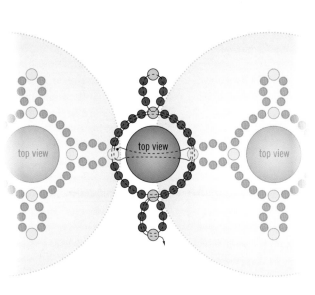

fig. 2

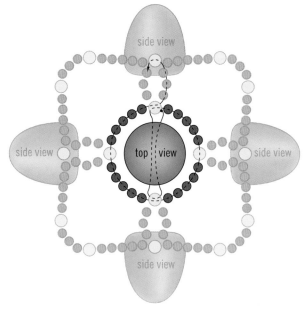

fig. 3

5 Work as in steps 2–4. but in step 3, skip the second repeat to create three gumdrop units in a row.

6 To join the beadwork into a ring, exit the end 11º from the last unit, pick up a gumdrop, and sew through the end 11º from the first unit. Retrace the thread path, and then work as in steps 2 and 3 to complete the gumdrop unit. Exit an open 11º at the end of a seed bead loop on one of the gumdrop units [**fig. 2**].

7 Add a gumdrop to the top: Pick up a gumdrop, and sew through the 11º at the end of the opposite seed bead loop. Sew back through the gumdrop and the 11º your thread exited at the start of this step. Pick up five 15ºs, and sew through the open 11º in the next seed bead loop. Repeat around the gumdrop, and then sew through the first three 15ºs and 11º of a seed bead loop [**fig. 3**].

8 Sew through the next two 15ºs of the same seed bead loop. Pick up an 11º, and sew through the center 15º of the five 15ºs next to the gumdrop just added. Pick up an 11º, and sew through the center 15º from the next seed bead loop. Repeat the last two stitches twice [**fig. 4**], and then retrace the thread path through the six new 11ºs added in this

step. Sew through the beadwork to exit the coordinating spot in the center of the next three gumdrops. Repeat this step three times, and then sew through to exit an open 11º on the other end of the bead.

9 Repeat steps 7 and 8 on this end of the bead. Retrace any loose sections, and end the thread.

10 For a necklace, make a total of three beaded beads.

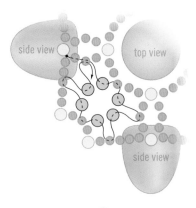

fig. 4

TO STRING THE NECKLACE

1 Cut 24 in. (61cm) of beading wire.

2 Crimp one half of the clasp to one end of the beading wire.

3 Pick up about 6¾ in. (17.1 cm) of peanut beads and a 15º.

4 String a 4mm bicone crystal, a 15º, five peanut beads, a 15º, a 4mm, and a Bumble Bead. Repeat twice, and then pick up a 4mm, a 15º, five peanut beads, a 15º, a 4mm, and a 15º.

5 Pick up about 6¾ in. (17.1 cm) of peanut beads.

6 Crimp the other end of the clasp to the end, and trim any excess wire.

Bugles with Crystals

I designed this beaded bead by combining many building-block elements into one stunning bead.

MATERIALS

- **24** 6mm twisted bugle beads, matte brown
- **24** 4mm bicone crystals, mocha
- **48** 3mm bicone crystals, olivine
- **24** 3mm bugle beads, matte olive green
- **6** 11º seed beads, matte brown
- 2 grams 15º seed beads in each of **2** colors: color A, transparent olive green; color B, metallic bronze
- Fireline, 6 lb. test
- Beading needles, #12
- Fabricated neckwire

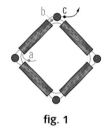

BEADS

- 4mm bicone crystal
- 3mm bicone crystal
- 4mm bugle bead
- 3mm bugle bead
- 11º seed bead
- 15º seed bead, color A
- 15º seed bead, color B

fig. 1

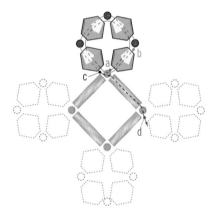

fig. 2

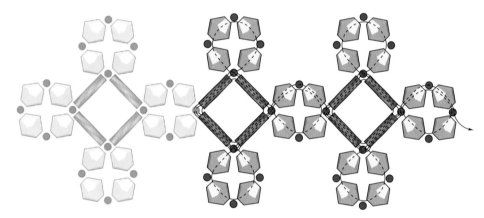

fig. 3

1 On 3 yd. (2.7m) of Fireline, pick up four 6mm bugle beads, leaving a 24-in. (61cm) tail, and sew through the first 6mm bugle picked up **[fig. 1, a–b]**. Pick up a color A 15º seed bead, and sew through the next 6mm bugle. Repeat the last stitch three times, and then sew through the next A **[b–c]**.

2 Pick up four 3mm bicone crystals, and sew through the A your thread exited at the start of this step and the first 3mm picked up in this step **[fig. 2, a–b]**. Pick up an A, and sew through the next 3mm. Repeat the last stitch two more times **[b–c]**, and then sew through the next A, 6mm bugle, and following A **[c–d]**. Repeat this step on the remaining A points of the bugle unit.

3 Working as in steps 1 and 2, make two more bugle units with crystal units on each corner using multiple thread paths (not shown), and exit the end **[fig. 3]**.

4 Join the strip by picking up two 6mm bugles, and sewing through the end A from the first unit. Pick up two bugles, and continue through the A your thread exited at the start of this step and the first bugle **[fig. 4]**. Pick up an A, and sew through the next bugle, A, and bugle. Repeat this stitch once, and then work as in step 2 to add the remaining crystal units to the top and bottom points of the bugle unit. Exit an open A of one of the crystal units between two bugle units.

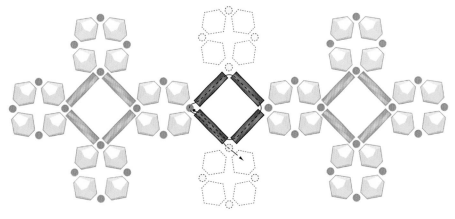

fig. 4

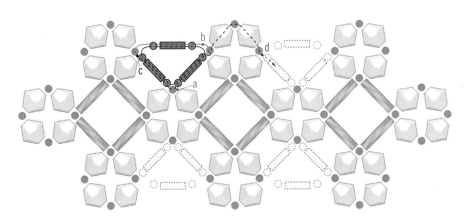

fig. 5

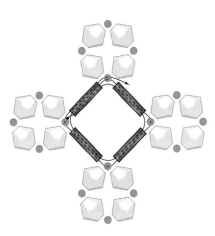

fig. 6

5 Pick up a color B 15° seed bead, a 3mm bugle, and a B. Sew through the next open A of the nearest crystal unit above a 6mm bugle unit **[fig. 5, a–b]**. Pick up a B, a 3mm bugle, and a B, and sew through the corresponding A from the crystal unit above the previous 6mm bugle unit **[b–c]**. Pick up a B, a 3mm bugle, and a B, and sew through the A your thread exited at the start of this step. Retrace the thread path, skipping the As. Sew through the beadwork to exit the side A of the next crystal unit **[c–d]**.

6 Work as in step 5 to add a 3mm bugle triangle unit between each 3mm crystal unit along each edge of the ring. Adding the 3mm bugle units will make the edges of the bead curve in. When you complete all eight 3mm bugle units, sew through the beadwork to exit the remaining open A at the top of a crystal unit.

7 Pick up a 6mm bugle bead, and sew through the next open A on this end. Repeat three times, and then retrace the thread path, skipping the As. Exit an A **[fig. 6]**.

Colors for this bead are the same as for the Design Option bracelet, p. 26. I left off the end crystal embellishments so the bead could slide over a thick chain or a beaded cord.

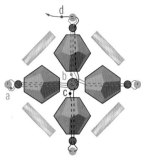

fig. 7

8 Work a 4mm bicone crystal embellishment on top of the 6mm bugle unit by picking up an A, a 4mm bicone crystal, an 11º seed bead, a 4mm, and an A, and sewing through the A opposite the A your thread exited at the start of this step. Sew back through the A, 4mm, 11º, 4mm, A, and the A your thread exited at the start of this step. Sew back through the first A, 4mm, and 11º picked up in this step **[Fig. 7, a–b]**.

9 Pick up a 4mm and an A, skip a 6mm bugle, and sew through the next open A. Sew back through the A, 4mm, and center 11º **[b–c]**. Repeat this step once, sew through the next 4mm and two As **[c–d]**, and end the working thread.

10 Using the other thread, sew through the beadwork to exit the open A on the opposite end of the bead. Repeat step 7, and then work as in steps 8 and 9 to add a 4mm crystal embellishment on the remaining 6mm bugle units.

11 Slide the beaded bead onto a fabricated neck wire. If you want to use a larger sized necklace or cord, omit the 4mm crystal embellishment on either end of the beaded bead.

DESIGN OPTION

Make a bangle bracelet by adding 6mm bugle and 3mm crystal units to the initial ring. On 3 yd. (2.7m) of thread, work as in steps 1 and 2 until you have enough units to fit around the largest part of your hand, and then join the beads into a ring as in step 4. Add the triangle bugle units as in step 5, but for the bugles along the edge of the bangle, use 6mm bugles instead of 3mm bugles. Finally, embellish the 6mm bugle units with 4mm crystals as in steps 8 and 9.

COLORS

- **90** 6mm twisted bugles, metallic bronze
- **60** 4mm bicone crystals, sand opal
- **180** 3m crystals, vintage rose
- **60** 3mm bugles, hybrid luster gold/green/rose
- **1 gram** 11º seed beads, lined topaz AB
- **15º seed beads:** color A, beige-lined crystal; color B, metallic bronze

Rings

Rizo Rings

*Weave cute flower components together,
and then connect them in a variety of ways
to make different ring tops.*

fig. 1

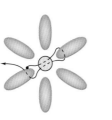

fig. 2

fig. 3

fig. 4

MATERIALS

Large ring
- **42** Rizo beads, jet Picasso
- **13** SuperDuo beads, jet Picasso
- **31** 8º seed beads, nickel
- 2 grams 15º seed beads, matte black
- Fireline, 6 lb. test
- Beading needles, #12

Small ring colors
- Rizo beads, jet Picasso
- SuperDuo beads, jet Picasso
- 8º seed beads, nickel
- 15º seed beads, matte black

1 On 18 in. (46cm) of Fireline, pick up six Rizo beads, leaving a 6-in. (15cm) tail. Sew through all the beads again to form a ring, and then sew through the first Rizo again [**fig. 1**].

2 Pick up an 8º seed bead, and sew through the opposite Rizo in the ring. Sew back through the 8º and the Rizo your thread exited at the start of this step [**fig. 2**].

3 Pushing all the tips of the Rizos to the front, work on the back of the flower. Pick up a 15º and sew through the next Rizo. Repeat five more times, and then sew through the first 15º picked up [**fig. 3**].

4 Pick up three 15ºs, and sew through the next 15º. Repeat five more times [**fig. 4**], and end the working thread and tail.

5 Repeat steps 1–4, but in step 4, don't complete the last stitch of three 15ºs. You'll connect the two components together at this point.

To connect the first two components:

For the last stitch, pick up a 15º, sew through the center 15º of the corresponding stitch of three 15ºs in another component, and then pick up a 15º. Sew through the next few 15ºs in the component your thread exited at the start of this step. Sew through the outer edge of 15ºs [**fig. 5**], and end the thread.

To connect components in shapes:

Connect the first two components as above. Work a component as in steps 1–4, but don't complete the last two stitches of three 15ºs. Instead, work as for connecting the first two components, but connect two points instead of one [**fig. 6**]. To make a ring with seven components, connect the 4th through 6th components as for a third component, and for the last component you'll connect three points instead of two [**fig. 7**].

NOTE: No matter what kind of ring design you are making, for the last component, start with a longer length of thread so you can make the ring band. If you are making a bracelet (see p. 30), just keep the tails of two of the components to make a loop of seed beads for a clasp.

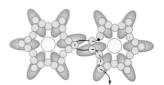

fig. 5

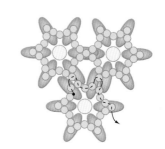

fig. 6

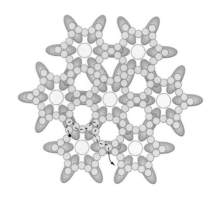

fig. 7

TO MAKE THE RING BAND

Exit a center 15º, and pick up a repeating pattern of an 8º and a SuperDuo until the ring band fits around your finger. Sew through a coordinating 15º on the opposite side of the components, and then back through all the beads just picked up. Sew through the beadwork to exit the next center 15º. Pick up an 8º, and sew through the open hole of the next SuperDuo. Repeat to add an 8º between the remaining SuperDuos, and then pick up an 8º, and sew through the corresponding 15º on the other side of the components. Sew back through this side of the ring band [figure], and end the thread.

figure

DESIGN OPTION

Connect a row of components by working as for the first two components in a straight line. For the first and last component, leave a tail long enough to make a small loop of seed beads to attach a clasp. Use a 3mm bicone crystal in place of the 8º seed bead in step 2 for added sparkle.

COLOR

- Rizo beads, amethyst azuro
- 3mm bicone crystals in place of 8º seed beads, light turquoise
- 15º seed beads, matte metallic blue iris

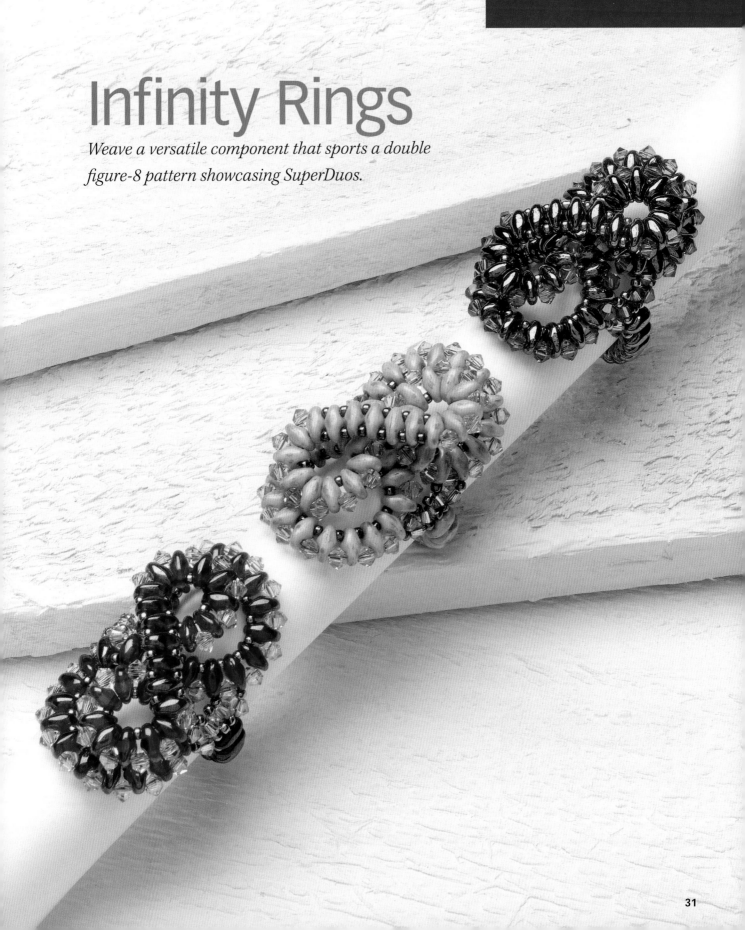

Infinity Rings

Weave a versatile component that sports a double figure-8 pattern showcasing SuperDuos.

MATERIALS

Purple ring

- **68** SuperDuo beads (53 for the ring top, approximately 15 for the band), matte ultra luster green

- **44** 3mm bicone crystals, light tanzanite

- 15º seed beads, hematite iris

- Fireline 6 lb. test

- Beading needles, #12

Green ring colors

- SuperDuo beads, hematite

- 3mm bicone crystals, olivine

- 15º seed beads, hematite iris

Red ring colors

- SuperDuo beads, Siam ruby vega

- 3mm bicones, crystal silver shade

- 15º seed beads, nickel electroplate

1 On 2 yd. (1.8m) of doubled Fireline, attach a stop bead, leaving a 6-in. (15cm) tail. Pick up a repeating pattern of a SuperDuo bead and a 15º seed bead six times, and then pick up a SuperDuo. Sew through the available hole of the last SuperDuo picked up, the first hole of this same SuperDuo, and then through the second hole again to change direction.

2 Pick up a 15º, and sew through the available hole of the next SuperDuo. Repeat until you have six 15ºs between the seven SuperDuos. Sew through the other hole of the SuperDuo your thread is exiting, and then sew through the beads along this edge, tying half-hitch knots between several of the beads, and exit the last SuperDuo in the row [**fig. 1**]. End the tail.

3 Pick up two SuperDuos, a 15º, three SuperDuos, a 15º, two SuperDuos, a 15º, and two SuperDuos. Pick up a repeating pattern of a 15º and a SuperDuo 16 times.

4 Sew through the available hole of the SuperDuo your thread is exiting, through the first hole again, and through the second hole to help keep the tension tight on the first side [**fig. 2**]. If at any time you have trouble keeping your tension, use this last stitch to help keep things from loosening up.

5 Pick up a 15º, and sew through the available hole of the next SuperDuo. Repeat this step for a total of three 15ºs.

6 Pick up a 3mm crystal, and sew through the available hole of the next SuperDuo. Repeat this step for a total of 22 3mms. Sew through the next six 15ºs and six SuperDuos to exit the end SuperDuo [**fig. 3**].

7 Pick up two SuperDuos, a 15º, three SuperDuos, a 15º, two SuperDuos, a 15º, and two SuperDuos. Pick up a repeating pattern of a 15º and a SuperDuo 12 times, and then pick up a 15º.

8 Connect the strand to the other end by sewing through the next SuperDuo, 15º, and SuperDuo on the side that has only three 15ºs on it. Sew through the other hole of the SuperDuo your thread is exiting, retrace the thread path through this SuperDuo again, and then exit out this side of the end section [**fig. 4**].

fig. 1

fig. 2

BEADS

- ⬡ SuperDuo bead

- ⬢ 3mm bicone crystal

- ● 15º seed bead

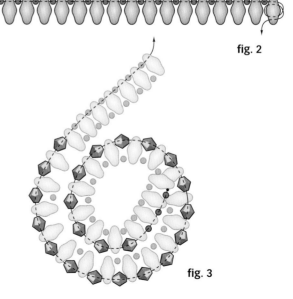

fig. 3

9 Pick up a 3mm, and sew through the remaining hole of the next SuperDuo. Repeat for a total of 22 3mms, and then end the thread. By the time you get to the 14th 3mm, you'll have to help form the figure-8 shape, but before you add the last crystal in this step, make sure the top of the figure 8 is totally formed. Your thread will have to be repositioned to exit the outside edge of the beads. Add the last 3mm, and end the thread.

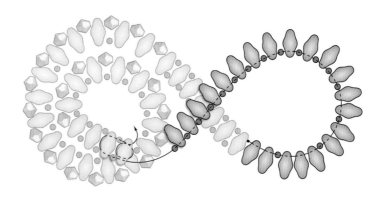

fig. 4

10 Double 24 in. (61cm) of Fireline, and add a stop bead, leaving a 6-in. (15cm) tail. Exit the second crystal along one edge of the bottom of the component at point **a**. Pick up a 15º, a 3mm, a 15º, a 3mm, and a 15º. Sew through the 3mm your thread exited on the component, and retrace the thread path several times. Exit the first 3mm picked up in this step [**fig. 5, a–b**].

11 Pick up a 15º, a 3mm, and a 15º. Sew through the 3mm your thread exited at the start of this step and the first 15º and 3mm picked up in this step [**b–c**].

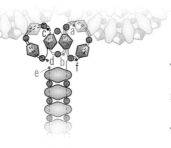

fig. 5

12 Pick up a 15º, and sew through a corresponding 3mm in the other loop along the same edge of the bottom of the component. Pick up a 15º, a 3mm, and a 15º, and sew through the 3mm added in the previous step. Continue through the 15º, 3mm, 15º, 3mm, and 15º [**c–d**]. End this thread.

13 Work as in steps 10–12 on the opposite side of the figure 8. Do not end this thread.

14 Pick up a repeating pattern of a SuperDuo and a 15º 14 times or until the band fits your finger. Sew through the corresponding 15º on the opposite side of the ring and the next two 15ºs. Sew through the available hole of the last SuperDuo, and pick up a 15º between each available hole of the SuperDuos. Sew through the two remaining 15ºs on the opposite end [**e–f**]. Retrace the thread path, and end the thread.

DESIGN OPTION

Make a multicolor component by working as above, but in step 1, make the first three SuperDuo beads a different color. After finishing step 6, work with this color again. To make a different color on the top layer, pick up 15 of the first color in step 1, and then finish up with the second color. In step 7, pick up ten SuperDuos in the first color, and then finish up with the second color.

COLORS

• SuperDuo beads: color A, red Picasso; color B, Siam ruby Picasso

• 3mm crystals, crystal silver shade

• 15º seed beads, nickel electroplate

Spinner Rings

Wrap a band of peyote stitch loose enough to spin around a ring base made with tubular herringbone. I like wearing this ring as a thumb ring, but you can easily make it fit any finger.

BEADS

☐ 10º Delica bead
☐ 11º Delica bead
● 15º seed bead

fig. 1

fig. 2

MATERIALS

Burgundy/nickel ring
- 2 grams 3mm bugle beads, matte brown iris
- 2–3 grams 10º Delica beads, nickel
- 1–2 grams 11º Delica beads, metallic burgundy
- 1–2 grams 15º seed beads, gunmetal iris
- Fireline 6 lb. test
- Beading needles, #12

Teal ring colors
- Bugle beads, matte teal iris
- 10º Delica beads, light green-lined clear AB
- 11º Delica beads, silk satin purple
- 15º seed beads, matte metallic teal

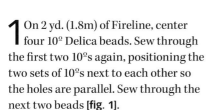

fig. 3

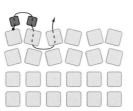

fig. 4

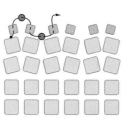

fig. 5

1 On 2 yd. (1.8m) of Fireline, center four 10º Delica beads. Sew through the first two 10ºs again, positioning the two sets of 10ºs next to each other so the holes are parallel. Sew through the next two beads [**fig. 1**].

2 Pick up two 10ºs, sew through the two 10ºs your thread exited at the start of this step, and the new 10ºs, making the new 10ºs sit parallel to the previous 10ºs [**fig. 2**].

3 Repeat step 2 until you have a strip long enough to fit around your finger, making sure you end up with an even number of beads in the round. Join the strip into a ring. Make a note of how many beads you used. My rings have 32 beads in the round to make 16 pairs for each herringbone stitch.

4 Working in modified herringbone stitch, pick up four 10ºs, and sew down through the next set of 10ºs in the ring, and up through the following set [**fig. 3**]. Repeat this step to complete the round, and step up through the first two 10ºs picked up in this step. Repeat along the opposite edge with the other thread.

5 Using either thread and working in herringbone, pick up two 11º cylinder beads and sew down through the next 10º in the round, and up through the next 10º [**fig. 4**]. Repeat to complete the round, and step up through the first 11º picked up in the round. Repeat this step along the opposite edge with the other thread. Exit one of the edge 10ºs.

6 Work a round behind the round of 11ºs picked up in the last step by picking up a 15º seed bead, and sewing down through the next 10º in the

round, and up through the following 10º. Repeat this step around this edge, pushing the pair of 11ºs added in the previous round to the front. Exit one of the 15ºs added in this round.

7 Pick up a bugle bead, and sew through the next 15º added in the previous step. Repeat to complete the round. Repeat this step along the opposite edge of the ring.

8 For the last round, pick up a 15º seed bead, and sew down through the next 11º in the round. Work an increase stitch by picking up a 15º, and sewing up through the next 11º in the round [**fig. 5**]. Repeat these two stitches to complete the round, and end this thread. Repeat this step along the opposite edge with the other thread.

Weave a smaller version of this design to make little components that work well for bracelets, necklaces, or earrings. Since the parts still spin, it makes these pieces a bit surprising.

To make a link instead of a ring:

1 Make a ladder as in steps 1–3, but work only six rows of ladder stitch (12 beads).

2 Work in herringbone stitch as in step 4 to complete the rounds on either side of the ladder base.

3 Using either thread and working in herringbone, pick up two 11º Delica beads and sew down through the next 10º in the round. Pick up a 15º, and sew up through the next 10º in the round. Repeat these two stitches to complete the round, and step up through the first 11º picked up in the round. Repeat this step along the opposite edge with the other thread.

4 For the edge rounds, pick up a 15º, and sew down through the next 11º in the round. Work an increase stitch by picking up two 15ºs, and sewing up through the next 11º in the round. Repeat these two stitches to complete the round, and end the thread. Repeat this step along the opposite edge with the other thread.

5 To make the spinner ring, work as in steps 8–9, but start by picking up a ring of 18 11ºs.

COLORS

- 10º Delica beads, nickel
- 11º Delica beads, metallic burgundy
- 15º seed beads, gunmetal iris

9 To make the spinner ring, on 1 yd. (.9m) of Fireline, center twice as many 11º cylinder beads as you picked up in step 3 to make the initial ring band. Sew through the first bead again, and slip this ring over the ladder ring. Make sure it spins easily, but doesn't fall off over the herringbone edges of the ring. Add or remove beads as needed, but make sure you end up with an even number of beads.

10 Hold the ring around the ladder base, and work a round of circular peyote using 11ºs, and step up through the first 11º picked up.

11 Work a round of peyote using 15ºs, and end this thread. Repeat this step on the opposite edge with the other thread.

Pyramid Rings

Tila beads stack into rings fit for a king or queen.
Crystals or pearls accent the lovely structure.

MATERIALS

Gold iris ring
- **8** Tila beads, gold iris
- **16** 3mm Swarovski pearls, light green
- 2–3 grams 11º seed beads, transparent raspberry rainbow
- 2 grams 15º seed beads, matte burgundy
- Fireline 6 lb. test
- Beading needles, #12

Purple ring colors
- Tila beads, green iris
- 3mm crystals instead of pearls, violet opal
- 11º seed beads, cobalt luster
- 15º seed beads: color A, matte metallic teal; color B, transparent light amethyst

BEADS

■ Tila bead

⬠ 3mm bicone crystal

● 11º seed bead

• 15º seed bead

fig. 1

fig. 2

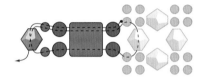

fig. 3

fig. 4

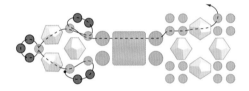

fig. 5

1 On 2 yd. (1.8m) of Fireline, pick up four 3mm pearls or bicone crystals. Sew back through the first 3mm to form a ring, leaving a 6-in. (15cm) tail. Retrace the thread path, exiting the first 3mm picked up.

2 Pick up a 15º seed bead and sew through the next 3mm in the ring. Repeat around the ring, and exit a 15º [**fig. 1**].

3 Pick up three 15ºs, and sew through the 15º your thread exited at the start of this step and the next 3mm and 15º in the ring. Repeat three times, and then sew through the next 15º in the ring and the first side 15º picked up in this step [**fig. 2**].

4 Pick up an 11º seed bead, a Tila bead, an 11º, a 15º, a 3mm, a 15º, and an 11º. Sew through the available hole of the same Tila just picked up, and then pick up an 11º. Sew through the nearest side 15º of the next loop of 15ºs and the 3mm in the ring between the two loops. Retrace the thread path through the side 15º, the 11º, the first hole of the Tila, the 11º, 15º, and end 3mm added in this step [**fig. 3**].

5 Pick up a repeating pattern of a 15º and a 3mm twice, and then pick up a 15º. Sew through the 3mm your thread exited at the start of this step, retrace the thread path of the beads just picked up, and exit the first 15º picked up in this step [**fig. 4**].

6 Referring to **fig. 5**, pick up two 15ºs, and sew through the 15º between the 11º and the 3mm at the bottom of the Tila, the 15º your thread exited at the start of this step, and the next 3mm and 15º in the new ring. Pick up three 15ºs, and sew through the 15º your thread just exited and the next 3mm and 15º in the ring. Sew through the next 15º (between the nearest 3mm and 11º), pick up two 15ºs, and sew through the 15º just exited in the ring. Sew through the next 15º, 11º, Tila, 11º, two 15ºs in the next loop, the 3mm in the ring, and the next side 15º in the following loop of 15ºs.

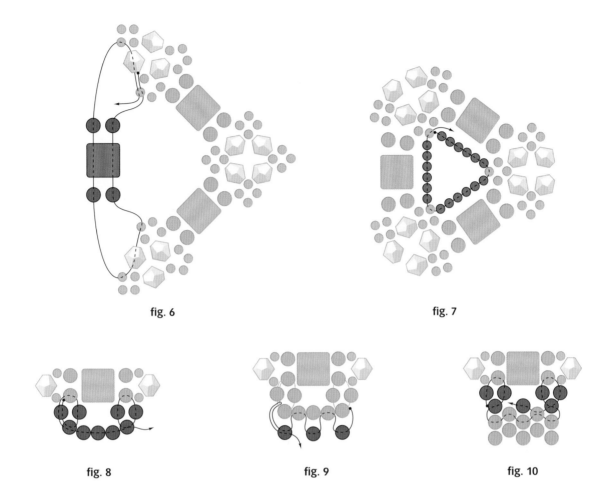

fig. 6

fig. 7

fig. 8

fig. 9

fig. 10

7 Repeat steps 4–6 three more times to complete a total of four spokes. Exit an open 3mm at the bottom of one of the spokes.

8 Connect the spokes of the pyramid by sewing through the nearest side 15°s in the next loop of 15°s. Pick up an 11°, a Tila, and an 11°. Sew through the corresponding side 15°, 3mm, and side 15° on the next spoke. Pick up an 11°, sew through the remaining hole of the Tila just picked up, pick up an 11°, and sew through the side 15° and 3mm on the first spoke [**fig. 6**]. Retrace the thread path, and then exit the corresponding spot on the spoke to connect the other spokes in the same manner. Exit one of the open 15°s in the center of a side triangle shape.

9 Pick up six 15°s, and sew through the next open 15° within the same triangle shape. Repeat two more times [**fig. 7**], and then repeat this step on the other three open triangle shapes. Exit an open 15° along the bottom edge of the pyramid. Work as in this step to add six 15°s between the four open corner 15°s. Exit one of the 11°s along this bottom edge.

10 Pick up three 11°s, and sew through the 11° your thread exited at the start of this step, and through the first two 11°s just picked up. Pick up five 11°s, and sew through the 11° at the other end of the same Tila. Pick up an 11°, and sew through the fourth 11° just picked up [**fig. 8**].

11 Work in odd-count peyote: Pick up an 11°, skip an 11°, and sew through the next 11°. Repeat twice, but for the last stitch, sew under the thread bridge between the two end 11°s and back through the last bead picked up [**fig. 9**].

12 Continue in odd-count peyote until your band is the desired length, and then connect the end row to the two end 11°s on the corresponding Tila opposite the 11° you started with. Exit an 11° in the end row, pick up an 11°, sew through the 11° next to the Tila, pick up another 11°, and sew through the 11° in the end row again. Repeat to connect the other end 11° [**fig. 10**]. Reinforce the join, and end the threads.

To make a pendant, work as in steps 1–12, but when you have about 16 rows, zip up the end row to the first row to make a bail. String the pendant on a cord or a beaded rope.

You can also use crossweave to make a Tila bead band for a ring: Center 2 yd. (1.8m) of Fireline on the inner hole of a bottom Tila, and cross the threads through a new Tila.

Pick up an 11º, a 15º, and an 11º on both threads. Cross the threads through the available hole of the same Tila. Cross the threads through a new Tila.

Repeat the previous step until you have the desired length. Cross the threads through the opposite bottom Tila. With both threads, sew through the beadwork to exit the 15ºs at the ends of the last Tilas. Pick up three 15ºs between each 15º, and end the threads.

COLORS

- Tila beads, olive gold luster
- 3mm pearls, light green
- 11º seed beads, black
- 15º seed beads, green/black-lined AB

Triangulation Rings

*Make amazing little components that stand up
and stand out in a fantastic ring.*

MATERIALS

Green ring

- **19** Tila beads, matte transparent green AB

- 8mm pearl, Swarovski light gold

- **4** 3mm pearls, Swarovski light gold

- 2 grams 11º seed beads, matte metallic dark green iris

- 2 grams 15º seed beads, matte metallic dark blue iris

- Fireline 6 lb. test

- Beading needles, #12

Blue ring colors

- Tila beads, transparent cobalt AB

- 8mm pearl, Swarovski light green

- 3mm pearls, Swarovski light green

- 11º seed beads, metallic blue-green iris

- 15º seed beads, metallic moss iris

Turquoise ring colors

- Tila beads, opaque turquoise green

- 8mm pearl, Swarovski white

- 3mm pearls, Swarovski white

- 11º seed beads, gold-lined aqua rainbow

- 15º seed beads, lime-lined luster

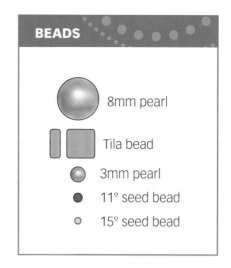

BEADS

8mm pearl

Tila bead

3mm pearl

11º seed bead

15º seed bead

fig. 1

fig. 2

1 On 2 yd. (1.8m) of Fireline, pick up a repeating pattern of three 11º seed beads and a Tila bead four times, leaving a 6-in. (15cm) tail. Sew through the first 11º to form a ring, and then retrace the thread path, skipping the center 11ºs to form a square. Exit a Tila **[fig. 1]**.

2 Sew through the available hole of the same Tila, and pick up three 11ºs between each available hole of the Tilas. Retrace the thread path, skipping the center 11ºs. Exit a Tila.

3 Pick up an 8mm pearl, sew through the opposite Tila, the next three 11ºs, and the following Tila. Sew through the pearl again, and then sew through the opposite Tila, the next three 11ºs, and the following Tila **[fig. 2]**. Retrace the thread path to secure the pearl in the center of the square.

4 With the thread exiting a Tila, pick up a 15º seed bead, a 3mm pearl, and a 15º. Sew back through the other hole of the same Tila your thread exited at the start of this step. Pick up a 15º, and sew back through the pearl just picked up. Pick up a 15º, and sew through the first hole of the Tila in this step **[fig. 3]**, the next three 11ºs in the square, and the first hole of the next Tila. Repeat this step to add a 3mm pearl embellishment to each Tila, and then exit a center 11º in the square.

5 Pick up an 11º, a Tila, an 11º, a 15º, an 11º, a Tila, and an 11º. Sew through the center 11º in the next corner of the square. Repeat around the square, and exit a Tila in the original square **[fig. 4]**. Sew through the other hole of the same Tila.

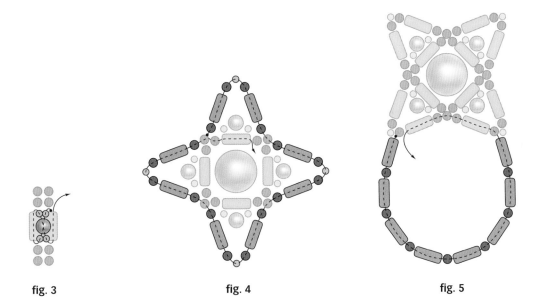

fig. 3   **fig. 4**   **fig. 5**

6 Pick up an 11°, sew through the available hole of the next Tila from step 5, pick up an 11°, a 15°, and an 11°, and sew through the available hole of the next Tila from step 5. Pick up an 11°, and sew through the next center 11° on this side. Repeat around, and then retrace the thread path through both sides, skipping the 15°s to define the points of each corner. Exit a side Tila and the 11° after it.

7 Pick up a repeating pattern of a Tila and an 11° seven times, and then pick up a Tila (or to the desired length to fit your finger). Sew through the coordinating 11° and Tila on the other side of the ring, the next three 11°s, and the Tila before the 11° your thread exited at the start of this step **[fig. 5]**. Sew through the other hole of the same Tila, and then sew through the beadwork to add an 11° to the available holes of the Tilas in the band. Retrace the thread path through the band, and end the thread.

To make a bracelet, see page 44.

Make the desired number of components (omitting the 8mm pearls) to make a bracelet, and add a cool, two-sided toggle clasp as a closure.

Exit a 15º at the corner of a component, pick up an 11º, a 3mm pearl, and an 11º, and sew through the corresponding 15º on another component. Sew back through the 11º, 3mm, 11º, and the 15º your thread exited at the start of this stitch [**fig. 1**].

Sew through the beadwork to exit the opposite side of these two components to attach the corner 15ºs in the same way. Attach the remaining components in the same way.

Make a double-sided toggle clasp to connect the end components:

On 1 yd. (.9m) of Fireline, pick up a Tila, an 11º, a 3mm pearl an 11º, a Tila, an 11º, a 3mm pearl, and an 11º, leaving a 6-in. (15cm) tail. Sew through the available hole of the second Tila picked up, and pick up an 11º. Sew through the 3mm pearl, pick up an 11º, and sew through the available hole of the first Tila. Pick up an 11º, a 3mm pearl, an 11º, and sew through the first hole of the first Tila.

Retrace the thread path, adding three 15ºs on each side of the center 3mm pearl, and a 15º between the 11º and 3mm pearl on each end [**fig. 2**].

Stitch a double layer by sewing through the end pearl, and picking up the same beads as for the first layer, but share the 3mms that are already in place instead of picking up new ones. Make a second double-layer toggle.

Exit a center 3mm pearl, and pick up about 1 in. (2.5cm) of beads, and sew through the center 3mm pearl on the second toggle. Retrace the thread path, and end the threads. Attach the toggle bars to the two end components to close the bracelet.

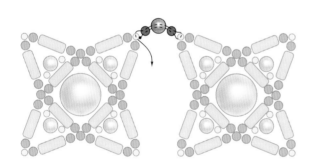

fig. 1

fig. 2

Earrings

Crystal Windows

*Work rounds of Tila beads, seed beads, and crystals
to make little geometric windows you can wear!*

1 On 1½ yd. (1.4m) of Fireline, pick up a repeating pattern of two 11º seed beads and a color A Tila bead four times, leaving a 6-in. (15cm) tail. Sew through the first 11º picked up to form a ring [fig. 1, a–b].

2 Pick up a 15º seed bead, and sew through the next three beads. Repeat this stitch three more times, and then sew through the next few beads to exit an A. Sew through the available hole of the same A to change direction [b–c].

3 Pick up two 11ºs, and sew through the available hole of the next A. Repeat this stitch three times, and sew through the first 11º picked up in this step.

4 Work as in step 2, but exit the first 15º picked up in this step. This is the bottom round of the inner ring.

5 Pick up two 11ºs, a color B Tila bead, and two 11ºs. Sew through the next 15º in the bottom round. Repeat this stitch three more times,

MATERIALS

- **16** Tila beads: **8** color A, bronze; **8** color B, silk satin cream
- **2** 6mm Swarovski cubes, olivine
- **8** 4mm Swarovski bicone crystals, crystal dorado
- **16** 3mm Swarovski bicone crystals, light topaz
- **8** 11º seed beads, gilt-lined opal
- **8** 15º seed beads, bronze
- Pair of earring findings
- Fireline 6 lb. test
- Beading needles, #12

BEADS

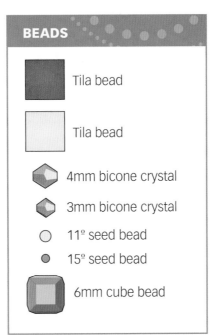

- Tila bead
- Tila bead
- 4mm bicone crystal
- 3mm bicone crystal
- 11º seed bead
- 15º seed bead
- 6mm cube bead

and then sew through the first 11º picked up in this step [fig. 2, a–b].

6 Pick up a 15º seed bead, and sew through the next three beads. Repeat this stitch seven more times, and then sew through the next few beads to exit a B. Sew through the available hole of the same B to change direction [b–c].

7 Pick up an 11º, a 3mm bicone crystal, an 11º, two 15ºs, an 11º, a 3mm, and an 11º, and then sew through the available hole of the next B. Repeat this stitch three more times, and then sew through the first 11º, 3mm, 11º, and 15º picked up in this step [fig. 3, a–b].

8 Pick up a 15º, and sew through the next nine beads in the outer ring. Repeat this stitch three more times, and then sew through the first 15º picked up in this step [b–c].

9 Pick up a 15º and a 4mm bicone crystal, and sew between the two sets of 11ºs and 15ºs to exit the center of the inner ring. Pick up a 15º, an 11º, a 6mm cube, an 11º, and a 15º, and sew between the corresponding sets of 11ºs and 15ºs on the opposite side of the inner ring. Pick up a 4mm and a 15º, and sew through the 15º at the point of the outer ring. Pick up a 15º, and sew back through the 4mm, 15º, 11º, 6mm, 11º, 15º, and 4mm. Pick up a 15º, and sew through the 15º at the point on this side of the outer ring. Sew through the next 11 beads along the outer ring to exit a 15º [fig. 4].

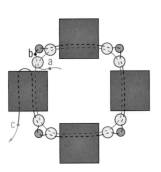

fig. 1

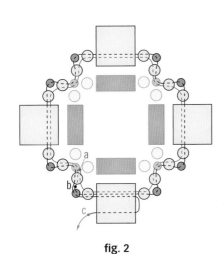

fig. 2

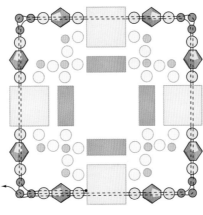

fig. 3

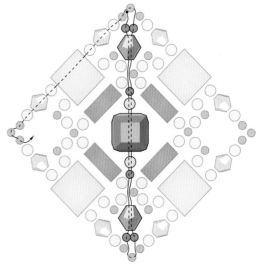

fig. 4

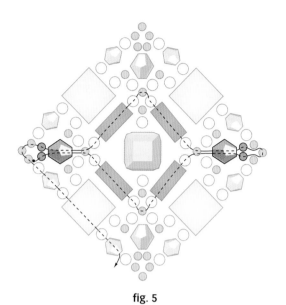

fig. 5

10 Pick up a 15° and a 4mm, and sew through the corresponding 15° and 11° along the inner ring, the bottom hole of the A, the 11°, 15°, 11°, the bottom hole of the next A, and the following 11° and 15°. Pick up a 4mm and a 15°, and sew through the 15° at the opposite point. Pick up a 15°, and sew back through the 4mm, 15°, the next inner 11°, A, 11°, 15°, 11°, A, and 11°. Sew through the 15° and the first 4mm picked up in this step, pick up a 15°, and sew through the 15° at this point along the outer ring. Sew through the next seven beads to exit a 3mm [**fig. 5**].

11 Pick up seven 15°s, and sew through the next 3mm in the outer ring to create a loop at the top of the earring. Retrace the thread path through the rounds until you reach the tail. Tie the threads in a knot, and end the threads.

12 Attach an earring finding to the loop of seed beads.

13 Make a second earring.

DESIGN OPTIONS

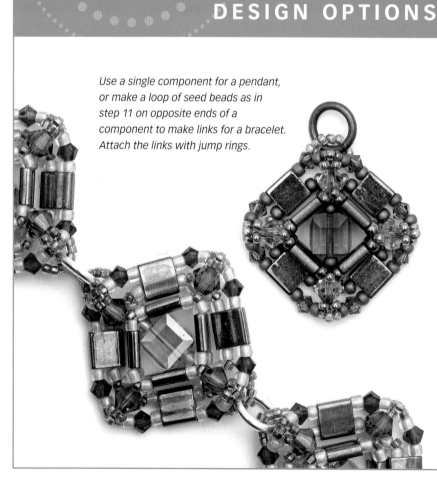

Use a single component for a pendant, or make a loop of seed beads as in step 11 on opposite ends of a component to make links for a bracelet. Attach the links with jump rings.

COLORS

Pendant
- Color A Tila beads, matte bronze
- Color B Tila beads, bronze iris
- 6mm Swarovski cubes, olivine
- 4mm Swarovski bicone crystals, crystal golden shadow
- 3mm Swarovski bicone crystals, olivine
- 11° seed beads, matte bronze iris
- 15° seed beads, transparent light green luster

Links
- Color A and B Tila beads, plum gold iris
- 6mm Swarovski cubes, light amethyst AB
- 4mm Swarovski bicone crystals, olivine
- 3mm Swarovski bicone crystals, ruby
- 11° seed beads, lined light green
- 15° seed beads, lined light amethyst amber

MATERIALS

Dark earrings

- **66** 3mm bugle beads, metallic bronze

- **14** 15º seed beads, metallic bronze

- Pair of earring findings

- Fireline, 6 lb. test

- Beading needles, #12

Light earring colors
- 3mm bugle beads, hybrid opaque lavender

- 15º seed beads, metallic bronze

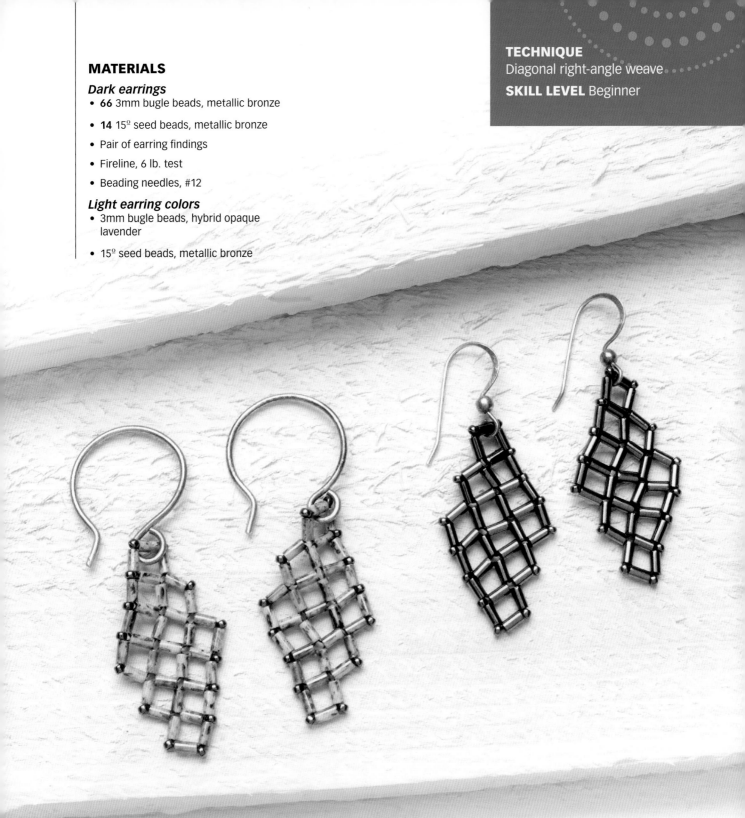

Bugle Diamonds

Make a few rows of diagonal right-angle weave into
delicate open earrings.

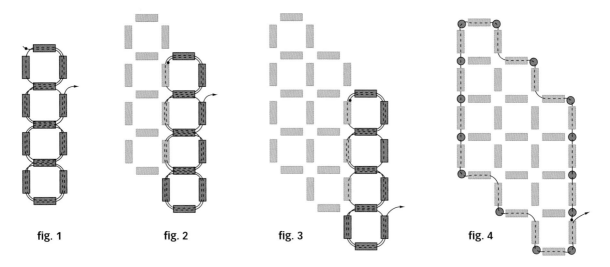

fig. 1   fig. 2   fig. 3   fig. 4

1 On 1 yd. (.9m) of Fireline, work a row of right-angle weave four stitches long using 3mm bugle beads, leaving a 6-in. (15cm) tail. Sew through the beadwork to exit the side bugle in the second stitch [**fig. 1**].

2 Work a row of four right-angle weave stitches off the first row using three bugles in the first stitch, two bugles in the next two stitches, and three bugles in the last stitch. Sew through the beadwork to exit the side bugle of the second stitch in the new row [**fig. 2**].

3 Repeat step 2 to make a third row of right angle weave off of the second, and exit the side bugle in the last stitch in this row [**fig. 3**].

4 Pick up a 15º seed bead, and sew through the next bugle. Repeat three times. On the jagged edges, pick up a 15º only along the outer edge of the bugles, and sew through the inner edge without picking up any 15ºs. Repeat around the edge [**fig. 4**]. End the thread.

5 Attach an earring finding to the first stitch in the first row.

6 Make a second earring.

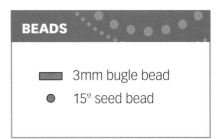

BEADS

▬ 3mm bugle bead

● 15º seed bead

DESIGN OPTION

Use 6mm twisted bugle beads to make a bracelet version. Create the desired number of rows, and then join them with another row of right-angle weave [**figure**].

Add 11º seed beads as in step 4, but only to the peaks.

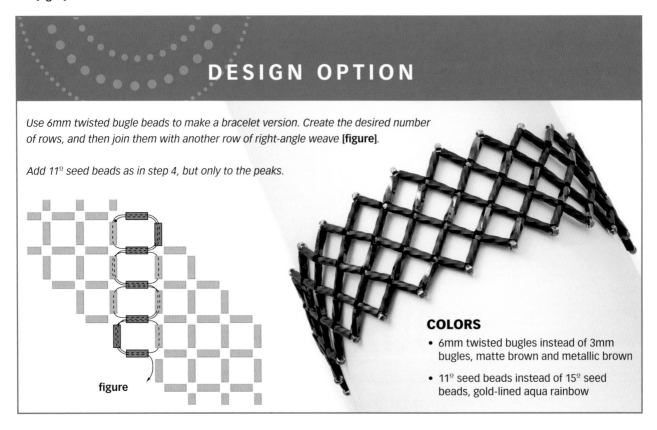

figure

COLORS
- 6mm twisted bugles instead of 3mm bugles, matte brown and metallic brown
- 11º seed beads instead of 15º seed beads, gold-lined aqua rainbow

Wonder Wheels

Create wonderful little pinwheel components to make earrings that hang from short lengths of chain.

BEADS

	SuperDuo bead
	4mm bicone crystal
	11º seed bead
	15º seed bead

MATERIALS

- **12** SuperDuo beads, opaque olive bronze vega
- **12** 4mm bicone crystals, olivine
- 2 grams 11º seed beads, gray/crystal AB
- 2 grams 15º seed beads, metallic olive
- 4–6 in. (10–15cm) small-link chain
- Pair of earring findings
- Fireline 6 lb. test
- Beading needles, #12
- Chainnose or flatnose pliers
- Wire cutters

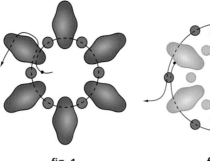

fig. 1

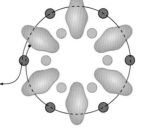

fig. 2

fig. 3

fig. 4

1 On 1½ yd. (1.4m) of Fireline, pick up a repeating pattern of a SuperDuo bead and an 11º seed bead six times. Sew through all the beads just picked up again, leaving a 12-in. (30cm) tail, and then sew through the first SuperDuo again. Sew through the available hole of the SuperDuo your thread is exiting to change direction [**fig. 1**].

2 Pick up an 11º, and sew through the available hole of the next SuperDuo in the ring. Repeat this step to add five more 11ºs [**fig. 2**]. Retrace the thread path to secure this side, and exit an 11º.

3 Pick up five 15º seed beads, and sew through the next 11º in the previous round. Repeat this step five more times [**fig. 3**]. Retrace the thread path of this round, skipping the center 15º of each stitch of five 15ºs to create sharp points. Set the working thread aside.

4 Using the tail and working off the 11ºs added in step 1, work as in step 3, and end the tail.

5 With the working thread, exit a center 15º, and pick up a 15º, a 4mm bicone crystal, and a 15º. Skip the center 15º opposite the 15º your thread is exiting, and sew through the next center 15º on the other side so the 4mm sits diagonally between two SuperDuos. Sew back through the 15º, 4mm, and 15º just picked up, and through the 15º your thread exited at the start of this

step. Sew through six beads to exit the next center 15º in the following stitch [**fig. 4**]. Repeat this step five more times. End the working thread.

6 Cut the chain into two equal lengths.

7 Slide a wheel onto one length of chain.

8 Open the loop on the earring finding, and attach the two end links of the chain onto the loop. Close the loop.

9 Make a second earring.

DESIGN OPTION

COLORS

- 8mm Swarovski pearls, crystal bronze
- 6mm bicone crystals, purple velvet
- SuperDuos, opaque olive bronze vega
- 11º seed beads, gray/crystal AB
- 15º seed beads, metallic olive

Make six or seven spacer beads by working steps 1–4 with these changes: In step 1, use 24 in. (61cm) of Fireline and in step 3, end the working thread. On 12 in. (30cm) of beading wire, string a crimp bead and half of a clasp at one end. Go back through, crimp the crimp bead, and trim the excess wire. String a 15º. String a repeating pattern of a 6mm bicone crystal, a 15º, an 8mm pearl, a 15º, a 6mm, and a spacer bead six or seven times. Then pick up a 6mm, a 15º, an 8mm, a 15º, a 6mm, and a 15º. String a crimp bead and the other half of the clasp, go back through, crimp, and trim the excess wire.

Sassy Spikes

Set large and small spike beads end to end in a netted
cage. Add a few crystals for sparkle.

MATERIALS

Hematite/bronze earrings
- **2** 6.5x16.5mm spike beads, gunmetal
- **2** 4.5x8mm spike beads, matte copper
- **8** 4mm bicone crystals, metallic light crystal
- Gram 15º Delica beads, gold iris
- Pair of earring findings
- Fireline 6 lb. test
- Beading needles, #13

Black/tan earrings
- 6.5x16.5mm spike beads, matte chalk bronze lumi
- 4.5x8mm spike beads, black
- 15º Delica beads, metallic steel

Black earrings
- 6.5x16.5mm spike beads, jet Picasso
- 4.5x8mm spike beads, black
- 15º Delica beads, metallic steel

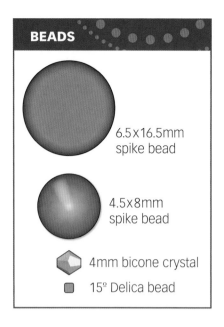

BEADS

6.5x16.5mm spike bead

4.5x8mm spike bead

4mm bicone crystal

15º Delica bead

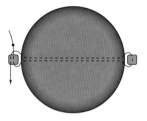

fig. 1

1 On 1 yd. (.9m) of Fireline, pick up a 15º Delica bead, a large spike bead, and a 15º, leaving a 6-in. (15cm) tail. Sew back through the large spike and the first 15º picked up so the tail and working thread are exiting opposite sides of the same bead [**fig. 1**].

2 Pick up 11 15ºs, and sew through the 15º on the opposite side of the spike. Repeat, and then retrace the thread path, skipping every sixth bead. Sew through the first six 15ºs picked up in this step [**fig. 2**].

3 Repeat step 2 [**fig. 3**].

4 Pick up a small spike bead, and sew through the 15º on the opposite side of the last step. Sew back through the small spike, the 15º your thread exited at the start of this step, and the next six beads [**fig. 4**].

5 Pick up a 15º, a 4mm bicone crystal, three 15ºs, a 4mm, and a 15º. Skip 11 15ºs in the last round, and sew through the next 15º Delica. Repeat this step, and sew through the first 15º, 4mm, and 15º picked up in this step. Skip a 15º, and sew through the next three beads [**fig. 5**].

6 Pick up three 15ºs, skip a 15º, and sew through the next 15º, 4mm, and 15º. Skip the next 15º, and sew through the next 15º, 4mm, and 15º. Pick up three 15ºs and sew through the next 15º. Sew through the beadwork to exit a 15º next to the hole of the small spike [**fig. 6**].

fig. 2

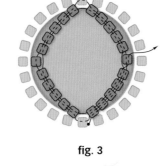

fig. 3

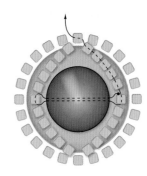

fig. 4

7 Pick up 11 15°s, sew through the 15° next to the hole on the opposite side of the small spike, and back through the last five 15°s picked up. Skip the next 15°, and sew through the first five 15°s picked up. Sew back through the 15° your thread exited at the start of this step, and end the thread.

8 Attach an earring finding to the loop of beads created in step 7.

9 Make a second earring.

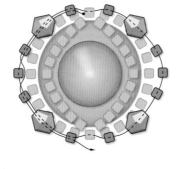

fig. 5

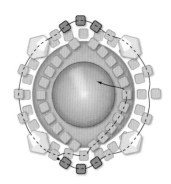

fig. 6

Starships

Two sizes of bugles create structures that are
slightly futuristic and totally cool.

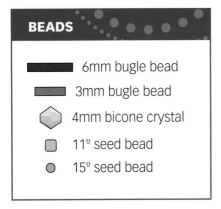

BEADS

▬ 6mm bugle bead

▭ 3mm bugle bead

⬡ 4mm bicone crystal

▢ 11º seed bead

● 15º seed bead

MATERIALS

- **16** 6mm bugle beads, black
- **40** 3mm bugle beads, jet Picasso
- **2** 4mm bicone crystals
- 2 grams 15º seed beads, nickel plated
- Gram 11º Delica beads, matte olive
- **2** jump rings
- Pair of earring findings
- Fireline, 6 lb. test
- Beading needles, #12

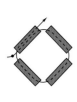

fig. 1

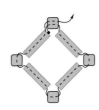

fig. 2

fig. 3

fig. 4

fig. 5

1 On 1½ yd. (1.4m) of Fireline, pick up four 3mm bugle beads, leaving a 12-in. (30cm) tail. Sew through the first 3mm bugle again [**fig. 1**].

2 Pick up an 11º cylinder bead, and sew through the next 3mm bugle. Repeat this step three times, and step up through the first 11º [**fig. 2**].

3 Pick up four 3mm bugles, and sew through the 11º your thread exited at the start of this step and the first 3mm bugle picked up. Pick up an 11º, and sew through the next 3mm bugle. Repeat the last stitch two more times. Skip the next 11º, and sew through the next 3mm bugle, 11º, 3mm bugle, and 11º [**fig. 3**].

4 Repeat step 3.

5 Repeat step 3 again, but instead of picking up the second 11º, sew through the end 11º from the first stitch to join the beads into a ring. Sew through the next 3mm bugle and 11º [**fig. 4**].

6 On each edge of the ring there are four open 11ºs. Join these 11ºs with 3mm bugles by picking up a 3mm bugle and sewing through the next open 11º. Repeat three times, and then retrace the thread path, skipping the 11ºs. Exit an 11º. Repeat on the other edge of the ring using the tail, and exit an 11º.

7 Working with the tail on the bottom diamond, pick up a 15º seed bead, a 6mm bugle, a 15º, a 4mm bicone crystal, and three 15ºs. Skip the three 15ºs just picked up and sew back through the 4mm. Pick up a 15º, a 6mm bugle, and a 15º, and sew through the next 11º in the diamond. Retrace the thread path of all the beads just picked up. Sew through the next few beads in the diamond to exit the next open 11º [**fig. 5**].

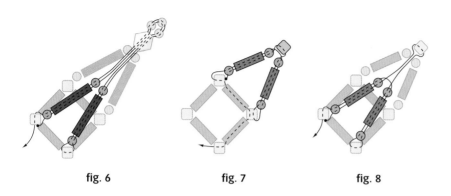

fig. 6   fig. 7   fig. 8

8 Pick up a 15º, a 6mm bugle, and a 15º. Sew through the 4mm, the three 15ºs, and back through the 4mm. Pick up a 15º, a 6mm bugle, and a 15º, and sew through the last open 11º in the diamond. Retrace the thread path of the new beads [fig. 6], and end the tail.

9 Using the working thread, make a 6mm bugle embellishment as in steps 7 and 8 with a loop for the earring finding by making the following changes: In step 7, pick up an 11º instead of a 4mm, and pick up seven 15ºs instead of three. Sew through the beadwork to exit an 11º in one of the diamonds in the circumference of the base bead.

10 Pick up a 15º, a 3mm bugle, a 15º, an 11º, a 15º, 3mm bugle, and a 15º. Sew through the next 11º in the diamond. Retrace the thread path through the beads just picked up, but skip the center 11º. Sew back through the 11º your thread exited in the diamond, and then sew through the beads in the diamond to exit the next open 11º [fig. 7].

11 Pick up a 15º, a 3mm bugle, and a 15º, and sew through the center 11º from the previous stitch. Pick up a 15º, a 3mm bugle, and a 15º, and sew through the remaining 11º in the diamond. Retrace the thread path through the beads just picked up, skipping the center 11º [fig. 8]. Repeat this step on the remaining three diamonds. End the thread.

12 Use a jump ring to attach an earring finding to the loop at the top of the earring.

13 Make a second earring.

DESIGN OPTION

Omit the top and bottom 6mm bugle bead embellishments to create a component. Use 4mm pearls as spacers and string them all together to make a crazy-cool bracelet.

COLORS

- 3mm bugle beads, matte teal blue iris
- 11º seed beads, higher metallic June bug
- 15º seed beads, higher metallic June bug

Cubes vs. Triangles

Create a rigid bracelet with rows of cube beads. Make an angle by using triangle beads, and then continue with cubes to form eight-sided bangles. These look great worn in a stack.

1 On 2–3 yd. (1.8–2.7m) of doubled Fireline, work in square stitch using 3mm cube beads to make a strip four beads wide and nine beads long [**fig. 1**], leaving a 6-in. (15cm) tail.

2 Work one row of square stitch using 3mm triangle beads.

3 Alternate nine rows of cubes with one row of triangles until you have eight of each, ending and adding thread as needed.

4 Join the ends together using a square-stitch thread path [**fig. 2**], and end the threads.

Gold iris bangle

Work as for the olive bracelet, but work a strip of beads three cubes wide and ten rows long in step 1. Alternate rows of three triangles with ten rows of three cubes until you have eight of each. Join using a square-stitch thread path, and end the threads.

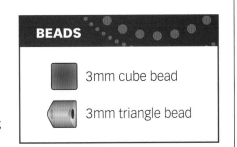

BEADS

3mm cube bead

3mm triangle bead

MATERIALS

Olive bangle (four beads wide) (10 in./25cm circumference)

- Approximately **320** 3mm cube beads, opaque matte olive green
- **32** 3mm triangle beads, matte metallic purple iris
- Fireline, 6 lb. test
- Beading needles, #10 or 12

Gold iris bangle colors

- 3mm cube beads, gold iris
- 3mm triangle beads, brown iris

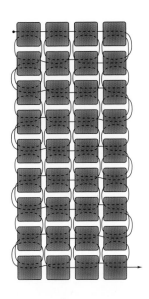

fig. 1

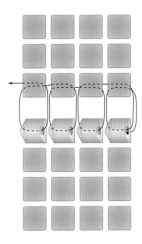

fig. 2

DESIGN OPTION

Switch out the cubes for triangles for a more organic version of this bangle. Since the triangles nestle together more than the cubes, work 13 rows of triangles instead of nine or ten to make the same size bracelet. Divide the eight triangle sections with stacks of cubes.

COLORS

- 3mm triangle beads, brown iris
- 3mm cube beads, gold iris

61

Stacked

Create a jagged and stylish design by stacking Tila beads at an angle. A bangle or a bracelet is the result, and wearing more than one causes quite a stir.

MATERIALS

Green bracelet (7 in./18cm)

- **48** Tila beads: **24** color A, metallic malachite green iris; **24** color B, matte metallic khaki iris

- **96** 3mm bugle beads, matte metallic green iris

- Clasp (optional)

- **2** jump rings (optional)

- Fireline, 6 or 8 lb. test

- Beading needles, #12

Black and gray bangle

- Tila beads

- Color A, matte black

- Color B, matte gray iris

- 3mm bugle beads, matte metallic nickel

fig. 1

fig. 2

fig. 3

1 On 3 yd. (2.7m) of 8 lb. single or 6 lb. doubled Fireline, pick up a color A Tila bead and a 3mm bugle bead, leaving a 6-in. (15cm) tail. Sew through the available hole of the A so the bugle sits on the edge of the A. Pick up a bugle, and sew through the first hole of the A again, the other bugle, and the second hole of the A [**fig. 1**].

2 Pick up a color B Tila bead, sew through the second hole of the previous A, and then sew through the first hole of the B [**fig. 2**].

3 Pick up a bugle, and sew through the available hole of the B. Pick up a bugle, and sew through the first hole of the B, the 3mm bugle, and the second hole of the B [**fig. 3**].

4 Work as in steps 2 and 3, alternating between A and B until you reach the desired length.

5 With the thread exiting a Tila, pick up three bugles, and sew through the last Tila. Retrace the thread path several times, and end the thread. Add half of the clasp to each end using a jump ring. To make a bangle instead, join the first and last Tila beads with the same thread path as in step 2, and end the thread. (I made an 8 in./20cm strip of beadwork for a bangle.)

Make a double-wide version of this bracelet. Make a single strip first as in steps 1–4, and then work as if making a second strip, but when you need to pick up a bugle along the edge, don't pick up a new bead, but rather sew through the corresponding bugle from the previous strip [figure]. Attach a two-strand clasp using four jump rings.

COLORS

- Tila beads: color A, olive gold luster; color B, plum gold luster
- 3mm bugle beads, metallic bronze

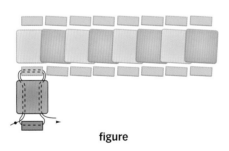

figure

Looming Layers

*Using a loom provides an interesting way to stitch up
this bracelet, but also provides a hand while stitching
the side embellishments. Tiles and rulla beads work
perfectly together to form a checkerboard pattern.*

MATERIALS

- **43** two-hole tile beads, opaque olive Picasso
- **86** Rulla beads, metallic olive
- 3 grams 10º Delica beads, metallic dark bronze
- 2 grams 15º seed beads, metallic olive
- 2-strand tube clasp
- Silamide or other nylon thread
- Beading needles, #12
- Loom

BEADS

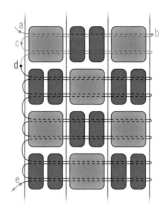

2-hole tile bead

Rulla bead

10º Delica bead

15º seed bead

fig. 1

New to loomwork? See p. 92 for an introduction.

1 Set up the loom with four warp threads.

2 Tie 2 yd. (1.8m) of Silamide to the first warp thread, pick up a tile, two Rullas, and a tile. Bring the beads up to the first warp thread, and push the beads up through the warp threads so you have one tile between two warp threads, two Rullas between the next two warp threads, and the last tile between the last two warp threads [fig. 1, a–b]. Making sure the needle is above the warp threads, sew back through the top holes of the beads [b–c].

3 Sew through the bottom holes of the beads, keeping the needle below the warp threads. Sew back through the bottom holes, keeping the needle above the warp threads [c–d].

4 Continue working as in steps 2 and 3, but alternate picking up a tile, two Rullas, and a tile with two Rullas, a tile, and two Rullas every other row [d–e]. End and add thread as needed. Make sure you end with a row of two tiles on each edge and two Rullas in the center stitch. Keep the beadwork on the loom until you finish the embellishments.

5 Thread a needle on both ends of 2 yd. (1.8m) of thread, and center it in the top holes of the first row of beads [fig. 2, a and aa].

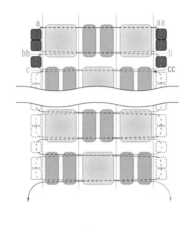

fig. 2

6 With each needle, pick up two 10º Delica beads, and then cross through the bottom hole of the beads in this row [a–b and aa–bb].

7 With each needle, pick up a 10º Delica bead, and then cross through the top holes of the beads in the next row [b–c and bb–cc].

8 Repeat steps 6 and 7 until you reach the end of the beadwork, and then sew back through the last 10º Delica bead on each edge of the beadwork.

9 With one needle, pick up a 15º seed bead, and sew through the next three 10º Delica beads along the same edge. Repeat with the other needle. Continue working along each edge until you reach the other end [fig. 3]. End the threads.

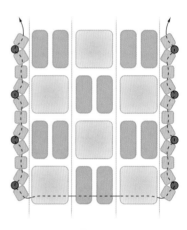

fig. 3

10 Cut the beadwork off of the loom, and end the two outer warp threads on each end.

11 With the two inner warp threads, attach the clasp with loops of seed beads: Pick up nine 15º seed beads, and sew through one of the rings on the clasp. Skip the last eight 15º's picked up, and then sew through the first 15º. Sew through the next two Rullas, and repeat the loop of 15º seed beads on the remaining ring of the clasp. End this thread. Retrace the thread path of the loops with the remaining thread on this end, and end the thread. Repeat this step on the other end of the beadwork.

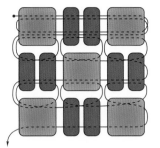

Another option: The bracelet can be worked in square stitch following this thread path.

DESIGN OPTION

Don't have a loom? You can work in crossweave to achieve the same look. Pick up the two-hole tile beads and the 10º Delica beads at the same time, then pick up a single 10º Delica on each thread and cross the threads through the two Rulla beads. Pick up two 10º Delica beads on each thread, and cross through the bottom holes on the Rullas [**fig. 1**]. *Join the beads into a ring using a crossweave thread path. Add the 15º seed bead embellishment along the edge as for the loomed bracelet* [**fig. 2**].

COLORS

- Tile beads, opaque olive Picasso
- Rulla beads, metallic olive
- 10º Delica beads, metallic olive
- 15º seed beads, metallic olive

fig. 1

fig. 2

Super-Slouchy Bangles

Working in Russian spiral with Tila beads makes easy entry points for each subsequent round. Nestling tiny cubes within the rounds creates a lush, fabric-like cuff that sits comfortably around the wrist.

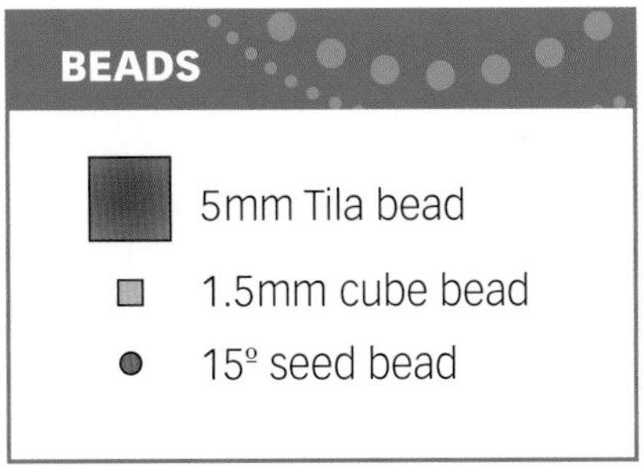

BEADS

■ 5mm Tila bead

▫ 1.5mm cube bead

● 15º seed bead

fig. 1

MATERIALS

Wide Tila bangle
(8 in./20cm circumference)

- **264** 5mm Tila beads, matte metallic light green

- 6–7 grams 1.5mm cube beads, matte metallic green/pink

- 4–5 grams 15º seed beads

- Fireline 6 or 8 lb. test, smoke

- Beading needles, #12

Narrow Tila bangle

- **177** 5mm Tila beads in two colors: **91** matte metallic gold iris (color A) and **86** gold iris (color B)

- 4–5 grams 1.5mm cube beads, matte metallic olive

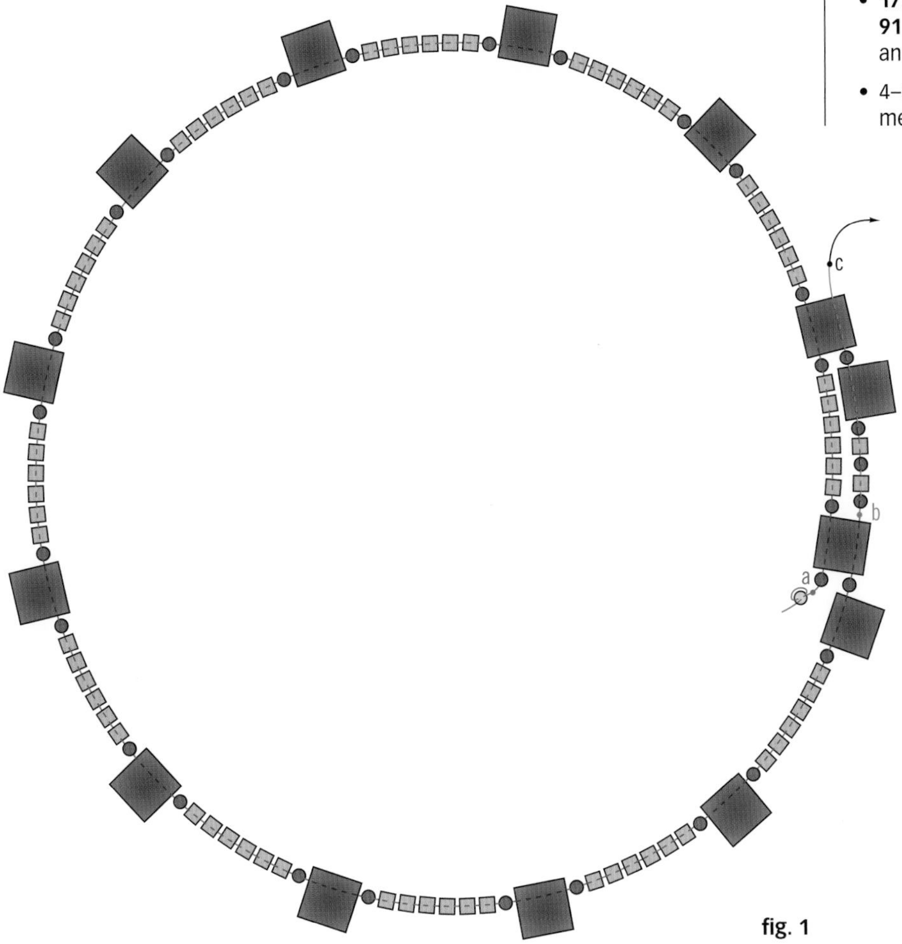

1 Thread a needle to the center of 4 yd. (3.7m) of Fireline so your working thread is 2 yds. (1.8m) doubled. Pick up a stop bead, leaving a 10-in. (25cm) tail.

2 Pick up a repeating pattern of a 15º seed bead, a Tila bead (if using two colors, start with color A), a 15º seed bead, and six 1.5mm cube beads 12 times, and then pick up a Tila and a 15º. Sew through the available hole of the first Tila to create a ring [**fig. 1, a–b**].

This ring should fit comfortably over the largest part of your hand. When measuring, make your hand as small as possible, as if sliding your hand through a bangle, so the bangle doesn't end up too large.

3 Keeping tight tension as you stitch, pick up a 15º, a cube, a 15º, a cube, a 15º, a Tila, and a 15º, and sew through the available hole of the next Tila in the ring [**b–c**]. Repeat this step 22 times for

If you have trouble getting a proper fit around the largest part of your hand in step 2, try changing the size or shape of beads used. You can use 11º seed beads in place of the 15º seed beads, or try a slightly larger bead in place of the 1.5 or 1.8mm cube beads.

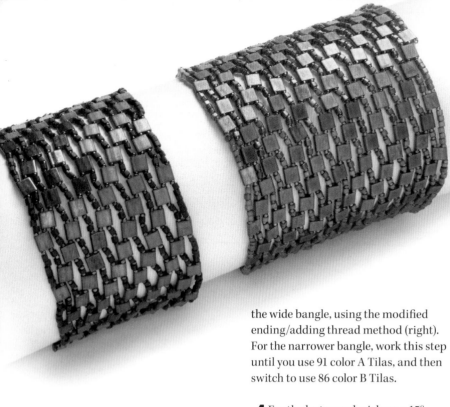

the wide bangle, using the modified ending/adding thread method (right). For the narrower bangle, work this step until you use 91 color A Tilas, and then switch to use 86 color B Tilas.

4 For the last round, pick up a 15º, six cube beads, and a 15º, and sew through the available hole of the next Tila in the previous round.

5 Pick up a 15º, sew back through the same hole your working thread just exited, and end the thread.

Ending/adding thread

Stop working when your thread is about 8 in. (20cm) long and attach a stop bead to hold the tension while you add the new length of thread.

Weave a new length of doubled thread several stitches or a row before the spot where your working thread left off, tying several half-hitch knots and exiting the spot where your working thread left off. Work a round with the new thread, and then attach a stop bead to hold the tension on the new thread. Remove the stop bead from the old working thread, tie off the remainder, and continue working with the new thread.

Repeat as needed to end and add new thread.

DESIGN OPTIONS

Make a less slouchy and more sparkly version of this bracelet using CzechMates two-hole tile beads, cubes, 15ºs, and 4mm bicone crystals. The first round is created by picking up a repeating pattern of a tile, a 15º, two cubes, a 15º, a 4mm, a 15º, two cubes, and a 15º 12 times, and then picking up a tile and a 15º. The second through fifth rounds consist of a 15º, a cube, a 4mm, a 15º, a tile, and a 15º per stitch. For the last round, pick up a 15º, two cubes, a 15º, a 4mm, a 15º, two cubes, and a 15º between the available holes of the tiles.

COLORS

- Tile beads, Picasso yellow
- 1.5mm cubes, amethyst gunmetal
- 15º seed beads, metallic olive

TECHNIQUES Modified right-angle weave, herringbone, netting
SKILL LEVEL Intermediate/advanced

Seedy Beady Bangles

Work layer upon layer to create an intricately patterned bangle. The variety of stitches allows a glimpse through to the texture and color below.

BEADS

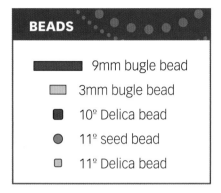

▬▬▬	9mm bugle bead
▭	3mm bugle bead
■	10º Delica bead
●	11º seed bead
▫	11º Delica bead

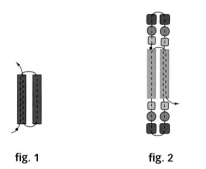

fig. 1   fig. 2    fig. 3

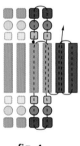

fig. 4

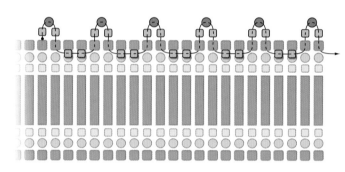

fig. 5

1 On 3 yd. (2.7m) of Fireline, center two 9mm bugle beads, and sew through the first 9mm bugle again so the two bugles sit side by side with their holes parallel [**fig. 1**].

2 Pick up an 11º Delica, an 11º seed bead, two 10º Delicas, an 11º seed bead, and an 11º Delica. Sew through the next 9mm bugle. Repeat this step, and then sew through the next 9mm bugle [**fig. 2**].

3 Pick up a 9mm bugle, and sew through the previous 9mm bugle and through the new bugle. Pick up a 9mm bugle, and sew through the previous bugle [**fig. 3**].

4 Repeat steps 2 and 3 [**fig. 4**] until you have a strip long enough to wrap around the largest part of your hand. Switch to the other thread when the working thread is about 6 in. (15cm). You need an even number of pairs of beads or the embellishment along the top of the base will not work out.

5 Join the beadwork into a ring by sewing through the end 9mm bugles several times. End the working thread and tail.

6 Add a new 2 yd. (1.8m) thread, and exit a 10º Delica along one edge of the bangle. Pick up an 11º Delica, an 11º seed bead, and an 11º Delica. Sew down through the next 10º Delica along the edge. Pick up two 11º Delicas, skip two 10º Delicas along the edge, and sew up through the next 10º Delica. The two 11º Delicas just picked up will push the skipped stack to the front, and the 11º Delicas should sit along the inner edge. Repeat this step along this edge [**fig. 5**], and then sew through the beadwork to repeat this step along the other edge.

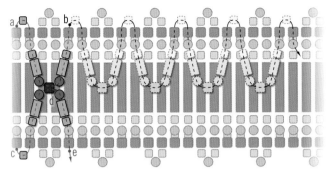

fig. 6

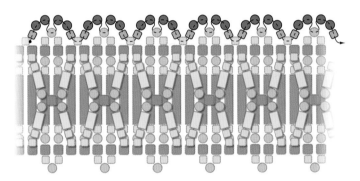

fig. 7

MATERIALS

Olive/brown bangle (front) *(8 in./20cm circumference)*

• 5 grams 9mm bugle beads, matte olive

• 3–4 grams 3mm bugle beads, matte gray iris

• 3–4 grams 10º Delica beads, metallic bronze

• 2–3 grams 11º seed beads, matte gray iris

• 2–3 grams 11º Delica beads, matte metallic light green

• Fireline 6 lb. test

• Beading needles, #12

Bronze/gold bangle colors

• 9mm bugle beads, metallic bronze

• 3mm bugle beads, green iris

• 10º Delica beads, matte bronze

• 11º seed beads, lined lime AB

• 11º Delica beads, gold iris

7 Sew through to exit a 10º Delica along the edge that was skipped in the last step. Pick up an 11º Delica, and sew down through the next 10º Delica and the 11º seed bead below it. Pick up an 11º Delica, a 3mm bugle bead, an 11º seed bead, a 10º Delica, an 11º seed bead, 3mm bugle, and an 11º Delica. Skip two 11º seed beads in the next stack, and sew up through the following 11º seed bead and 10º Delica above it **[fig. 6, a–b]**. Repeat this step along this edge of the bangle. Sew through the beadwork to exit the corresponding 10º Delica along the other edge.

8 Pick up an 11º Delica, and sew up through the next 10º Delica and the 11º seed bead above it. Pick up an 11º Delica, a 3mm bugle, and an 11º seed bead, and sew through the center 10º Delica from the opposite stitch picked up in step 7 **[c–d]**. Pick up an 11º seed bead, 3mm bugle, and an 11º Delica. Skip two 11º seed beads in the next stack, and sew down through the following 11º seed bead and 10º Delica below it **[d–e]**. Repeat this step along this edge, and end the thread.

9 Add 2 yd. (1.8m) along one edge of the bangle, and exit an 11º Delica added in the previous round. Pick up an 11º Delica and two 11º seed beads. Sew through the 11º seed bead in the next stack along the edge. Pick up two 11º seed beads and an 11º Delica, and sew through the 11º Delica in the next stack. Continue in this manner around this edge **[fig. 7]**. Retrace the thread path, skipping the 11º Delicas and 11º seed beads not picked up in this step to form a sharp zigzag along the edge. Sew through the beadwork to repeat this step on the other edge. End the threads.

DESIGN OPTION

Make a narrower version of the bangle with 3mm bugle beads in place of the 6mms. When you get to steps 7–9, omit the 3mm bugle bead.

COLORS

- 3mm bugle beads, hybrid luster gold smoky topaz rose and green

- 10º Delica beads, metallic burgundy

- 11º seed beads, transparent Montana gold luster

- 11º Delica beads, metallic blue/burgundy

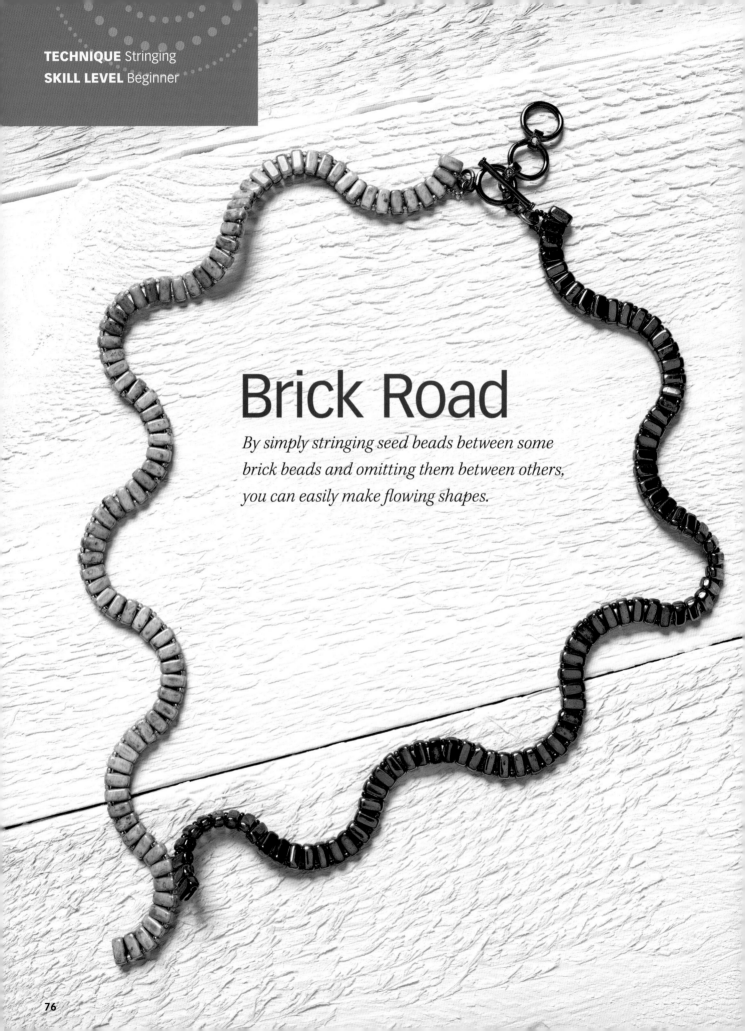

Brick Road

By simply stringing seed beads between some brick beads and omitting them between others, you can easily make flowing shapes.

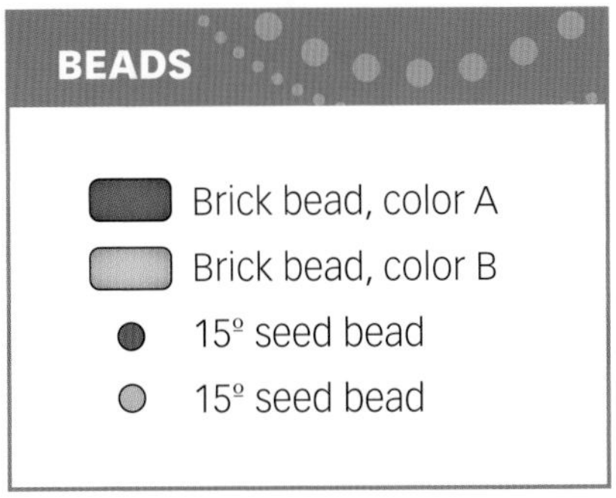

BEADS

- █ Brick bead, color A
- ▭ Brick bead, color B
- ● 15° seed bead
- ● 15° seed bead

1 On 2 yd. (1.8m) of Fireline, pick up a stop bead, and center it on your thread. Pick up 10 color A brick beads. Pick up an alternating pattern of a color A 15° seed bead and an A brick until you have 10 A 15°s, ending with a 15° **[fig. 1]**. Repeat these two stitches until you have five sections with 10 bricks and four sections with 15°s and nine bricks. Attach a stop bead to the end of this thread.

2 Remove the stop bead from the center of the thread, and using this side of the thread, sew through the available hole of the end brick. Pick up a 15°, and sew through the available hole of the next brick. Continue until you reach the 10th brick. This will make the section curve to the left **[fig. 2, a–b]**.

3 Sew through the next nine bricks to make the next section curve to the right **[b–c]**.

4 Continue working as in steps 1 and 2 until you reach the end of the sections.

5 Remove the stop bead, and using the other thread, sew through the other hole of the brick your thread is exiting and the next four beads to exit the third brick on this side of the beadwork **[fig. 3, a–b]**.

6 Using the other thread, sew through the first three beads on the other end of the beadwork. Make a loop for the clasp by picking up nine 15°s, and then sew through the same brick again **[c–d]**. Retrace the thread path several times, and end this thread. Save the other thread to join the two halves of the necklace.

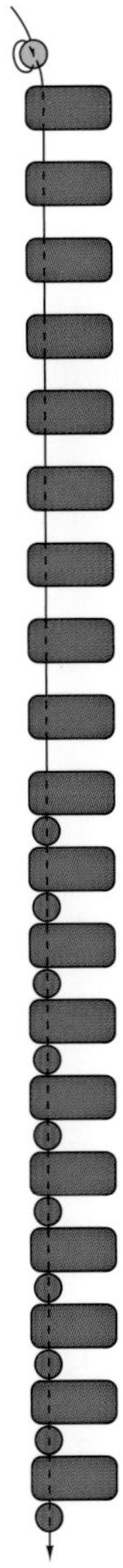

fig. 1

MATERIALS

Necklace (19 in./48cm)

- Brick beads: **86** color A, brown iris; **86** color B, opaque ultra luster green
- 2 grams 15° seed beads in each of two colors: color A, metallic brown; color B, transparent light green luster
- Clasp
- 2 jump rings
- Fireline 6 lb. test
- Beading needles, #12

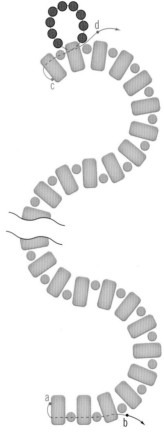

fig. 3

fig. 2

77

7 Repeat steps 1–5 using color B bricks.

8 Align the two halves so the tail from the first half meets up with the eighth B brick. Sew through the B brick and back through the A brick **[fig. 4]** several times until the connection is secure. End this thread.

9 Using the remaining thread from the color B half of the necklace, sew through the beadwork to exit the corresponding bead to add the loop for the clasp. Work as in step 6.

10 With a jump ring, attach half the clasp to the loop. Repeat for the other half.

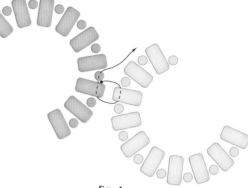

fig. 4

DESIGN OPTION

I used Rulla beads in place of bricks to make a wavy bracelet rendition of this design. Work eight sections as in steps 1–4, and then join the ends of the Rulla beads. Retrace the thread path, and end the threads. Make a second wavy ring, and use the threads to connect the second ring to the first as in step 8. I picked a spot on the first and second wavy rings, and attached them at the same spot four different times, working around the rings. Repeat with a third wavy ring if desired.

COLORS

- Rulla beads: color A, blue turquoise bronze Picasso; color B, black

- 15º seed beads, hybrid light beige Picasso

Spiraling SuperDuos

*Spiral around and around until you reach the middle,
and then turn around and spiral right back again.
This makes a beautiful necklace that really shows
off those special SuperDuo beads.*

MATERIALS

Necklace (18½ in./46cm)

- 4mm bicone crystals: **120** color A, chrysolite satin; **120** color B, sand opal
- **360** SuperDuos, opaque luster Picasso
- 4–5 grams 11º seed beads, matte metallic dark green
- 3–4 grams 15º seed beads, hybrid light beige Picasso
- Clasp
- **2** jump rings
- Fireline 6 lb. test
- Beading needles, #12
- Beading thread wax

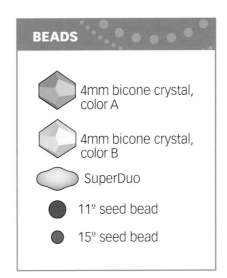

BEADS

- 4mm bicone crystal, color A
- 4mm bicone crystal, color B
- SuperDuo
- 11º seed bead
- 15º seed bead

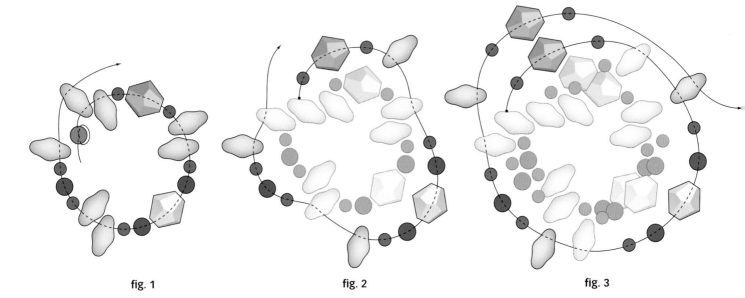

fig. 1   fig. 2   fig. 3

1 On 2 yd. (1.8m) of doubled and waxed Fireline, pick up a stop bead, leaving a 12-in. (30cm) tail. Pick up two SuperDuos, a 15º seed bead, a color A 4mm bicone crystal, a 15º, two SuperDuos, a 15º, an 11º seed bead, a color B 4mm crystal, an 11º, a 15º, two SuperDuos, a 15º, an 11º, a 15º, and a SuperDuo. Sew through the available hole of the first SuperDuo to form a ring [**fig. 1**]. The second SuperDuo in each pair will get flipped up out of the way for now. If necessary, thread the tail through the available hole of the second SuperDuos to help keep them out of the way.

2 Pick up a 15º, an A, a 15º, and a SuperDuo. Skip four beads in the previous round, and sew through the available hole of the next SuperDuo. Pick up a 15º, an 11º, a B, an 11º, a 15º, and a SuperDuo. Skip six beads in the previous round, and sew through the available hole of the next SuperDuo. Pick up a 15º, an 11º, a 15º, and a SuperDuo. Skip four beads in the previous round, and sew through the available hole of the next SuperDuo.

3 Repeat step 2 until you reach 9 in. (23cm) or the desired halfway point of the necklace, ending and adding thread as needed. Be sure to complete step 2 before moving on to the next step.

4 To change direction and create a V at the center of the necklace: Pick up a 15º, an A, and a 15º, and sew through the next SuperDuo. *Pick up a SuperDuo, a 15º, an 11º, a B, an 11º, and a 15º. Sew through the next SuperDuo. Pick up a SuperDuo, a 15º, an 11º, and a 15º, and sew through the next SuperDuo. Pick up a SuperDuo, a 15º, an A, and a 15º. Sew through the available hole of the first SuperDuo added in this round [**fig. 3**].

5 Repeat step 4 from the * until you have the same length on this side as on the first side.

6 Work the last round as before, but omit the SuperDuos. Retrace this round, and exit a SuperDuo. Pick up nine 15°s, and sew through the SuperDuo your thread just exited. Retrace the thread path of the loop, and then sew through the beadwork to exit the next SuperDuo. Repeat the loop of 15°s, and end the thread. Remove the stop bead, and repeat this step with the tail on the other end of the necklace.

7 With a jump ring, attach half of the clasp to the two loops of 15°s on one end of the necklace. Repeat on the other end.

You'll change direction to create this center V shape in step 4.

DESIGN OPTION

Using 3 yd. (2.7m) of doubled thread, make a matching bangle by working steps 1–3 until you have a spiral large enough to fit over the widest part of your hand. Join the ends by aligning the SuperDuos in the first and last rounds. (Using different colors of SuperDuos makes this join easier. I also used 10° Delicas in place of 11° seed beads in the third stitch of step 2.)

Join the ends by first completing the first two stitches of step 2:
- *Pick up a 15°, a 10°, and a 15°. Sew through the corresponding SuperDuo from the first round. Sew through the next SuperDuo in the last round.*

- *Pick up a 15°, an A, and a 15°. Sew through the corresponding SuperDuo from the first round. Sew through the next SuperDuo in the last round.*
- *Pick up a 15°, an 11°, a B, an 11°, and a 15°. Sew through the corresponding SuperDuo from the first round. Sew through the next SuperDuo in the last round.*
- *Pick up a 15°, a 10°, and a 15°. Sew through the SuperDuo next to the stop bead. Remove the stop bead, and end the working thread and tail.*

COLORS

- 4mm bicone crystals: color A, mocha; color B, sand opal

- SuperDuos: color A, matte ultra luster green; color B, turquoise bronze Picasso; color C, Siam ruby Picasso

- 10° Delica beads (in place of 11°s in the third stitch of step 2), matte metallic green iris

- 11° seed beads, gold-lined aqua rainbow

- 15° seed beads, permanent galvanized dark steel

Tila Links

Trusty Tila beads are wonderful for their uniform shape. Create lively little links with a tiny bit of sparkle on each corner. A long chain is so light, it is an easy-to-wear accessory.

BEADS

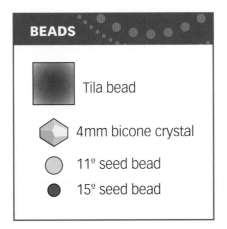

Tila bead

4mm bicone crystal

11º seed bead

15º seed bead

MATERIALS:

Necklace (19 in./48cm)

- **188** Tila beads, metallic malachite green iris

- **188** 3mm bicone crystals, light tanzanite

- 4–5 grams 11º seed beads, transparent gray luster

- 4–5 grams 15º seed beads, gunmetal iris

- Fireline 6 lb. test

- Beading needles, #12

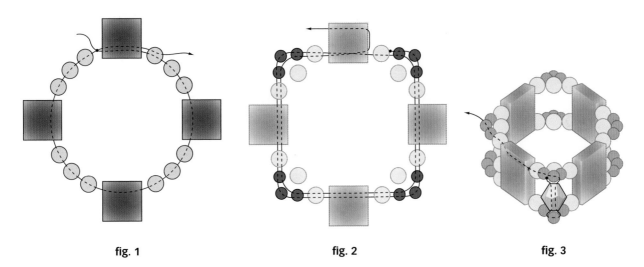

| fig. 1 | fig. 2 | fig. 3 |

1 On 24 in. (61cm) of Fireline, pick up a repeating pattern of a Tila bead and three 11º seed beads four times, leaving a 6-in. (15cm) tail. Tie the beads into a ring with a surgeon's knot. Sew through the first Tila and 11º picked up in this step [**fig. 1**].

2 Pick up three 15º seed beads, skip an 11º, sew through the next 11º, and continue through the next Tila and 11º. Repeat this stitch three more times, and then retrace the thread path, skipping the center 15ºs to make the beads form pointed corners. Exit a Tila, and change direction by sewing through the available hole of the same Tila [**fig. 2**].

3 Pick up three 11ºs, and sew through the available hole of the next Tila. Repeat this step three more times, and then work as in step 2, but exit one of the center 15ºs.

4 Pick up a 3mm bicone crystal, and sew through the center 15º opposite the 15º your thread just exited. Sew back through the 3mm and the 15º your thread exited at the start of this step. Sew through the next 15º, 11º, Tila, 11º, and two 15ºs [**fig. 3**]. Repeat this step three times, and end the threads.

5 For subsequent links: Work as in steps 1–4, but before tying the beads into a ring in step 1, sew through the center of the first ring. Repeat until you have 46 links or reach the desired length.

Use CzechMates two-hole tile beads instead of Tila beads, 10º Delica beads instead of 11º seed beads, and 3mm pearls instead of 3mm crystals to make this slightly chunkier bracelet. Make a ring of 24 15ºs and attach a clasp.

COLORS

- CzechMates two-hole tile beads, opaque olive Picasso
- 3mm Swarovski pearls, light green
- 10º Delica beads, metallic olive green
- 15º seed beads, gunmetal iris

Petal Perfect

Peyote stitch unites petal beads in perfect beaded flowers. You can do so many things with them!

MATERIALS

Necklace (20 in./51cm)

- **25** large (13x14mm) rose petal beads, opaque teal/bronze
- **30** small (7x8mm) rose petal beads, light green/bronze
- **4–5** grams 11º seed beads, matte dark green
- **3–4** grams 15º seed beads: color A, green-lined AB; color B, bronze
- Clasp
- **12** in. (30cm) chain
- **4** jump rings
- Fireline 6 lb. test
- Beading needles, #12

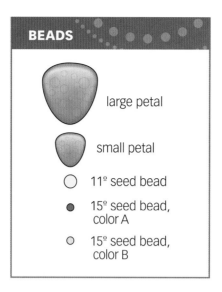

BEADS

large petal

small petal

◯ 11º seed bead

● 15º seed bead, color A

○ 15º seed bead, color B

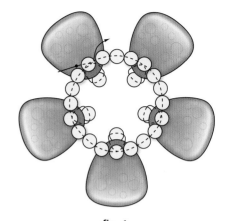

fig. 1
(front view)

Large flower component

1 On 2 yds. (1.8m) of Fireline, center an 11º seed bead, a large rose petal bead from front to back, and an 11º. Sew back through the large petal. Sew through the first 11º picked up so the working thread and tail are exiting opposite ends of the 11º.

2 Pick up four 11ºs, a large petal from front to back, and an 11º. Sew back through the large petal. Sew through the 11º picked up just before the petal bead. Repeat this step three more times for a total of five large petals.

3 Pick up three 11ºs and sew through the first 11º picked up on the top of the first large petal to form a ring [**fig. 1**]. Sew down through the first large petal and the 11º below it.

4 On the back of the component, pick up three 11ºs and sew through the 11º below the next large petal. Repeat this step four more times to create a ring [**fig. 2**].

5 Work a round of peyote by picking up an 11º, skipping an 11º in the ring, and sewing through the next 11º. Repeat to complete the round, and then step up through the first 11º picked up in this step [**fig. 3**].

6 Pick up three 11ºs, and sew through the next 11º in the previous round. Pick up an 11º, and sew through the next 11º in the previous round. Repeat these two stitches to complete the round, and sew through the beadwork to exit an 11º along the inner ring in the center of the petals [**fig. 4, a–b**].

7 Work a round of peyote using color B 15º seed beads, and step up through the first two 15ºs picked up in this step [**b–c**].

8 Pick up a B, and sew through the next two Bs in the previous round. Repeat to complete the round, and step up through the first B picked up in this step [**c–d**].

9 Work a round of peyote using 11ºs by picking up an 11º, skipping the two Bs sewed through in the previous round, and sewing through the next B. Repeat to complete the round [**d–e**]. Sew through to the outer round of the seed beads and exit the center 11º in a three-bead unit. Use this thread to connect the components.

10 On the front of the component, using the other thread, work a round of peyote using Bs and flipping them toward the inner circle. Step up through the first B picked up in this step.

11 Pick up a B, and sew through the next two Bs in the previous round. Repeat to complete the round, and step up through the first B picked up in this step.

12 Work a round using 11ºs by picking up an 11º, skipping the two Bs sewed through in the previous round, and sewing through the next B. Repeat to complete the round [**fig. 5**], and end the thread.

13 Repeat steps 1–12 to make a total of five large flower components.

Small flower component

14 On 1 yd. (.9m) of Fireline, center a color A 15º seed bead, a small rose petal bead from front to back, and an A. Skip the last A picked up, and sew back through the small flower petal. Sew through the first A picked up so the working thread and tail are exiting opposite ends of the A.

15 Pick up four As, a small petal bead from front to back, and an A. Skip the last A picked up, and sew back through the small petal. Sew through the A picked up just before the small petal. Repeat this step three more times to make a total of five small petal beads.

fig. 2
(back view)

fig. 3
(back view)

Center bead
of 3-bead unit

a

b

d

e

c

fig. 4
(back view)

fig. 5
(front view)

back view

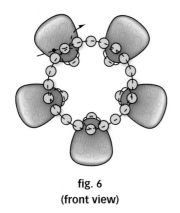

fig. 6
(front view)

fig. 7
(back view)

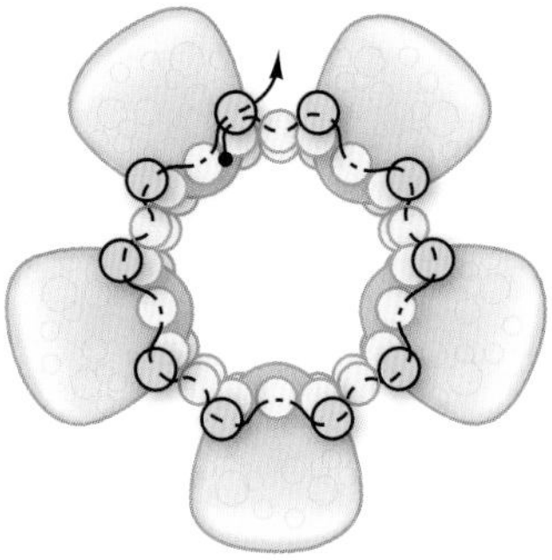

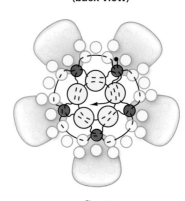

fig. 8
(back view)

fig. 9
(back view)

fig. 10
(front view)

fig. 11
(front view)

16 Pick up three As, and sew through the first A picked up on the top of the first small flower petals to form a ring [fig. 6]. Sew down through the first small flower petal and the A below it.

17 On the back of the component, pick up three As and sew through the A below the next small petal bead. Repeat this step four more times to create a ring [fig. 7].

18 Work a round of peyote by picking up an A, skipping an A in the ring, and sewing through the next A. Repeat to complete the round, and then step up through the first A picked up in this step [fig. 8].

19 Pick up three As, and sew through the next A in the previous round. Pick up an 11º seed bead, and sew through the next A in the previous round. Repeat these two stitches to complete the round, and sew through to exit an 11º [fig. 9]. Save this thread to connect the components.

20 On the front of the component, using the other thread, work a round of peyote by picking up an A, skipping A in the ring, and sewing through the next A. Repeat to complete the round [fig. 10], and then sew through an A in the inner ring of the flower petals.

21 Pick up a color B 15º, and sew through the next two As in the inner ring. Repeat to complete the round, and step up through the first B picked up in this step.

22 Work a round using 11ºs by picking up an 11º and sewing through the next B. Repeat to complete the round. Sew through all five 11ºs [fig. 11], and end the thread.

23 Repeat steps 14–22 to make a total of six small flower components.

24 Lay out the components on your work surface until you have a pleasing arrangement. Connect the components by exiting an 11º on one component, picking up five 11ºs, and sewing through a corresponding 11º on another component. Pick up five 11ºs, and sew through the 11º your thread exited on the first component. Retrace the thread path several times, and then end the thread. Continue to connect all the components together in this way.

25 Make a loop on each end of the connected flower components to attach the chain: Exit an 11º on a component, pick up eleven 11ºs, and sew through the 11º your thread exited on the component. Retrace the thread path and end the thread. Attach half of the chain to each end loop with a jump ring.

26 Attach half of the clasp to each chain end with a jump ring.

Use these versatile flower components to make necklaces, bracelets, earrings, or rings.

To make a large piece such as a necklace or bracelet, arrange the components on your work surface and connect them as in step 24.

To make loops to attach earring findings, follow step 25.

To make a ring, exit an 11º on a component, make a loop of 11ºs to fit your finger, and then sew through a bead on the opposite side of the component. Reinforce with several loops, or work peyote stitch off the ring to make a larger band. End the thread.

Earrings
- Small rose petals, light green/bronze
- 11º seed beads, light green-lined rainbow
- 15º seed beads: color A, rainforest matte metallic iris; color B, transparent light green luster

Bracelet
- Large rose petals, opaque teal/bronze
- Small rose petals, light green/bronze
- 11º seed beads, matte dark green
- 15º seed beads: color A, green-lined AB; color B, bronze

COLORS

Ring
- Large petals, red/bronze luster
- 11º seed beads, gold-lined rainbow
- 15º seed beads, brown iris

Necklace
- Small rose petals: color A, matte red luster; color B, transparent red luster
- 15º seed beads: color A, transparent red rainbow; color B, matte metallic gold

STRINGING & WIREWORK

Crimping

Use crimping pliers and crimp beads to secure the ends of flexible beading wire:

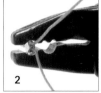

1 Position the crimp bead in the notch closest to the handle of the crimping pliers. Hold the wires apart to make sure one wire is on each side of the dent, and squeeze the pliers to compress the crimp bead.

2 Position the crimp bead in the notch near the tip of the pliers with the dent facing the tips. Squeeze the pliers to fold the crimp in half. Tug on the wires to make sure the crimp is secure.

Opening and closing plain loops, jump rings, and earring findings

1 Hold a loop or a jump ring with two pairs of pliers.

2 To open the loop or jump ring, bring the tips of one pair of pliers toward you, and push the tips of the other pair away from you. Reverse the steps to close.

Making a plain loop

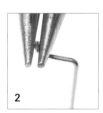

1 Using chainnose pliers, make a right-angle bend approximately ¼ in. (6mm) from the end of the wire.

2 Grip the tip of the wire with roundnose pliers. Press downward slightly, and rotate the wire into a loop. The closer to the tip of the pliers you work, the smaller the loop will be.

3 Let go, then grip the loop at the same place on the pliers, and keep turning to close the loop.

Making a wrapped loop

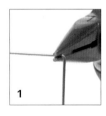

1 Using chainnose pliers, make a right-angle bend approximately 1¼ in. (3.2cm) from the end of the wire.

2 Position the jaws of the roundnose pliers in the bend.

3 Curve the short end of the wire over the top jaw of the pliers.

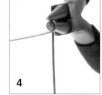

4 Reposition the pliers so the lower jaw fits snugly in the loop. Curve the wire downward around the bottom jaw of the pliers. This is the first half of a wrapped loop.

5 To complete the wraps, grasp the top of the loop with chainnose pliers.

6 Wrap the wire around the stem two or three times. Trim the excess wire, and gently press the cut end close to the wraps with chainnose pliers.

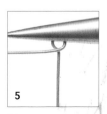

BEAD STITCHING

Stop bead

Use a stop bead to secure beads temporarily as you begin stitching. Choose a bead that is distinct from the beads in your project. String the stop bead, and sew through it again in the same direction. For extra security, sew through it again.

Adding and ending thread

To add thread, sew into the beadwork several rows prior to the point where the last bead was added. Weave through the beadwork, following the existing thread path. Tie a few half-hitch knots between beads, and exit where the last stitch ended. To end a thread, weave back into the beadwork, following the existing thread path and tying two or three half-hitch knots between beads as you go. Change directions as you weave so the thread crosses itself. Sew through a few beads after the last knot, and trim the thread.

Half-hitch knot

Pass the needle under the thread between two beads. A loop will form as you pull the thread through. Cross back over the thread between the beads, sew through the loop, and pull gently to draw the knot into the beadwork.

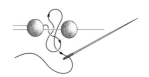

Square knot

Bring the left-hand thread over the right-hand thread and around. Cross right over left, and go through the loop.

Surgeon's knot

Bring the left-hand thread over the right-hand thread twice. Pull the ends to tighten. Cross right over left, and go through the loop. Tighten.

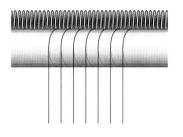

fig. 1

LOOMWORK

Warping the loom

1 Tie the end of a spool of thread to a screw or a hook at one end of the loom.

2 Guide the thread between two coils of the spring and across to the other end of the loom. Guide the thread between the corresponding coils of the opposite spring, and wrap it around the screw or hook at this end. Go back over the spring, placing the thread in the next coil. Cross over to the first end of the loom, placing the thread in the corresponding coil, and wrap it around the screw or hook. Note: If you are using beads that are larger than 11º seed beads, you may want to skip one or more coils between warp threads.

3 Continue wrapping the thread between coils, keeping the thread a bead's width apart **[fig. 1]**, until you have one more warp thread than the number of beads in the width of the pattern. Keep the tension even, but not too tight. Tie the last warp thread to a hook or screw on the loom, and cut the thread from the spool.

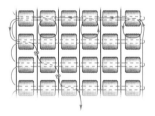

fig. 2

Finishing the loomwork

1 To remove the beadwork from the loom, carefully cut the warp threads as close to the screw or hook as possible.

2 Starting with the end warp on one side, thread a needle, and sew through the first bead in the end row. Sew through the corresponding bead in the adjacent row, the first bead again, and the next bead or two in the row. Repeat, moving down the end row. At the end of the row, sew into the beadwork, and end the thread **[fig. 2]**.

3 Repeat with the remaining warp threads, moving away from the end row as you end each thread.

4 Repeat on the other end with the remaining warp threads, making sure to maintain even tension throughout the strip of loomwork. If you pull too hard, the beads will bunch up.

HERRINGBONE STITCH

Tubular

1 Work a row of ladder stitch (see "Ladder stitch: Making a ladder") to the desired length using an even number of beads. Form it into a ring to create the first round (see "Ladder stitch: Forming a ring"). Your thread should exit the top of a bead.

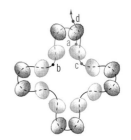

2 Pick up two beads, sew down through the next bead in the previous round **[a–b]**, and sew up through the following bead. Repeat to complete the round **[b–c]**.

3 You will need to step up to start the next round. Sew up through two beads — the next bead in the previous round and the first bead added in the new round **[c–d]**.

4 Continue adding two beads per stitch. As you work, snug up the beads to form a tube, and step up at the end of each round until your rope is the desired length.

LADDER STITCH

Making a ladder

1 Pick up two beads, and sew through them both again, positioning the beads side by side so that their holes are parallel **[fig. 1, a–b]**.

fig. 1

2 Add subsequent beads by picking up one bead, sewing through the previous bead, then sewing through the new bead **[b–c]**. Continue for the desired length.

fig. 2

This technique produces uneven tension, which you can correct by zigzagging back through the beads in the opposite direction **[fig. 2]**, or by using the "Crossweave method" below.

Crossweave method

1 Thread a needle on each end of a length of thread, and center a bead.

2 Working in crossweave technique, pick up a bead with one needle, and cross the other needle through it **[a–b and aa–bb]**. Add all subsequent beads in the same way.

Forming a ring

With your thread exiting the last bead in the ladder, sew through the first bead, and then sew through the last bead again.

PEYOTE STITCH

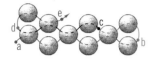

Flat even-count

1 Pick up an even number of beads **[a–b]**. These beads will shift to form the first two rows.

2 To begin row 3, pick up a bead, skip the last bead picked up in the previous step, and sew back through the next bead **[b–c]**. For each stitch, pick up a bead, skip a bead in the previous row, and sew through the next bead, exiting the first bead picked up **[c–d]**. The beads added in this row are higher than the previous rows and are referred to as "up-beads."

3 For each stitch in subsequent rows, pick up a bead, and sew through the next up-bead in the previous row **[d–e]**. To count peyote stitch rows, count the total number of beads along both straight edges.

Tubular

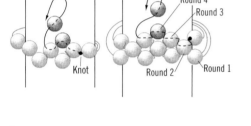

Tubular peyote stitch follows the same stitching pattern as flat peyote, but instead of sewing back and forth, you work in rounds.

1 Start with an even number of beads in a ring.

2 Sew through the first bead in the ring. Pick up a bead, skip a bead in the ring, and sew through the next bead. Repeat to complete the round.

3 You need to step up to be in position for the next round. Sew through the first bead added in round 3. Pick up a bead, and sew through the second bead in round 3. Repeat to achieve the desired length.

Zipping up or joining

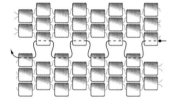

To zip up (join) two sections of a flat peyote piece invisibly, match up the two end rows and zigzag through the up-beads on both ends.

RIGHT-ANGLE WEAVE

Flat strip

1 To start the first row of right-angle weave, pick up four beads, and tie them into a ring (see "Square knot"). Sew through the first three beads again.

2 Pick up three beads. Sew through the last bead in the previous stitch **[a–b]**, and continue through the first two beads picked up in this stitch **[b–c]**.

3 Continue adding three beads per stitch until the first row is the desired length. You are stitching in a figure-8 pattern, alternating the direction of the thread path for each stitch.

Acknowledgments

*I would like to thank my family, especially my
parents and my children, for their patience and
support. As always, I thank my readers and fans,
whose interest in my work keeps me creating.*

ABOUT ANNA

Anna Elizabeth Draeger is a well-known jewelry designer, former
associate editor for *Bead&Button* magazine, and the author of
the books *Crystal Brilliance*, *Great Designs for Shaped Beads*,
and *Crystal Play*. Since 2009, Anna has been an ambassador
for the Create Your Style with Swarovski Elements program, a
handpicked worldwide network of artists who are known for their
design expertise and passion for teaching.

Anna's website is originaldesignsbyanna.squarespace.com. You
can contact Anna at beadbiz@mac.com or visit her Etsy store
annaelizabethdraeger.etsy.com.

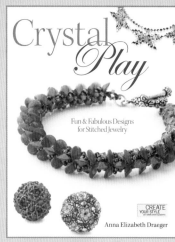